The DNA
of a
Christian Soul

The DNA
of a
Christian Soul

Your Christ Identity

ASISAT LAMINA

RESOURCE *Publications* · Eugene, Oregon

THE DNA OF A CHRISTIAN SOUL
Your Christ Identity

Resource Publications
An Imprint of Wipf and Stock Publishers
199 W. 8th Ave., Suite 3
Eugene, OR 97401

www.wipfandstock.com

PAPERBACK ISBN: 978-1-5326-8278-0
HARDCOVER ISBN: 978-1-5326-8279-7
EBOOK ISBN: 978-1-5326-8280-3

Manufactured in the U.S.A.   MARCH 3, 2020

Contents

CONTENTS

Preface

PRIOR TO WRITING THIS book, my journey with Christ could easily be summed up by the passage below:

> *"He sat me down at his table*
> *He laid his hand upon my head*
> *He said, "My child, my daughter, you are truly blessed*
> *I've waited eternities to caress your head*
> *For you to know the weight and flight of my breath,*
> *I poured you out in pages, when nations went astray, I measured out your talents so in you they'd find a way*
> *I watched the devil taunt you, I had to turn my head, coz for you to take the victory you had to take my bread . . .*
> *My daughter, you had to raise your head*
> *To know from whence creation was fed.*
> *You fought with cloak and dagger*
> *You fought in pain and dread*
> *You hated me with passion, but you always sought my bed*
> *You thought me a dictator, a master, you the slave*
> *And in your hate you served me, without knowing all my names.*
> *I visited on you such dangers that caused all you knew to flee*
> *But I showed you all my glory—from my head, my back, and feet*
> *I burdened you with promise, so you would never go astray, but I also held back its being while I cleared away all shame.*
> *I showed you all my archives, and the heavens, which are mine*
> *And I know you won't believe it, but I created you for these times*

Some people strive in greatness, but daughter you've borne your load

Now step into your greatness—I've washed away death's clothes.

Love, your Father, God"

I never really understood why being a Christian was so hard. I knew God was real and I believed everything he said, but nothing in my life reflected any of his promises in the Bible. I was confused; I was disheartened; I thought I was the only one—I thought I was going crazy. Surely there couldn't be anything wrong with God, so there had to be something wrong with me. I read so much, tried so much, learned so much about Christ, but nothing seemed to really shift or change. Then I finally found the answer. God's truths were wrapped up and hidden within different fragments of my identity and soul. Unfamiliar pieces and divine realities were simply misaligned, tangled up, and out of sync. There was nothing wrong with me. I stepped into Christ's full DNA the moment I answered his call—we all did. We all just simply forgot to go back to school to find out who we'd really become in Christ. Unravelling the habits and traits of our old DNA and stepping into the new gives a voice to the unspoken, common narrative of our Christian experiences. It pours out our internal dialogues and watches Christ step in to reorganize and realign what we thought were hopeless messes and expired dreams. Our God is so, so faithful—what he's put inside you will blow your mind!

Knowing Who's In Control

THIS IS ABOUT ACCEPTING the absolute truth of who God is, and of knowing he is in total control of everything and everyone.

God doesn't just have power over Christians, but over every human that has lived; over every government; over the weather; over the oceans and waves, and over all the forces of darkness and evil.

God has no rival or equal, and the devil is not his archenemy. They are not matched, so there is absolutely no competition. God is the uncreated one; he created everything, including the devil.

God gave all humans free will and, in the beginning, dominion and power over all the earth, including all things spiritual and physical. In the garden, Adam and Eve gave their power to Satan. And that is the power that Satan operates with—he has none of his own. When we accept the calling of Jesus, that power is reinstated back to us, through God's sovereign will.

The devil works by deceiving and manipulating us into believing he still has power over us—that is a lie. And this is what the Bible is here for, to put us in constant remembrance of our position in Christ, our dominion in Christ, and our inheritance in Christ.

God has complete and utter and total control. The last two verses of Isaiah 54 tell us that even the weapons that the devil tries to use against us were originally created by God. That is why we can take comfort in the scriptures that tell us no weapons formed against us can prosper.

There has only ever been one creator: our Father, God. At his best, the devil can mimic things that have already been created. But he is powerless to make anything new, because there is only one God.

This opening chapter is really about understanding this critical foundation—that God is God all by himself. He reigns in all majesty and power, and he is elevated far above all the works of his hands, above all people and nations, above every angel and demon. Lord of all and Lord over all.

Let's prepare our hearts and minds to receive and acknowledge this truth. It's the knowledge of his sovereign power that allows us to revere him, honor him, and be led by him.

Amen

Lord, You Will Not Be Denied Your Glory

I didn't do anything; you chose me before I was formed
I didn't know anything; you molded me in your forge
I couldn't bring anything; you carried me in your wings
I wouldn't be anything unless I'd confess you as king.

Your arm of mighty thunder yet tender as a lamb
You strike the waves asunder and declare you are, I AM
You are the Great Deliverer, The Lion, and The Rose
You are the world's redeemer, you cast away death's clothes.

In you we find a healer, a servant, and a friend
You are our soul's protector, our beginning, and the end
You are the peace provider; you carried all our woes,
Our griefs and cares have vanished with every heavy yoke.

You are the everlasting, the only way to life
Your truth is all sustaining, you cannot be denied
We will confess your glory, your power, Lord most high
The earth will bow before you and receive you in your might.

We will push back the darkness, as commanded from your throne
We will destroy the evil—your authority shall be known
We will uproot the mountains and tear the idols down—
wickedness will be plucked up and principalities drowned.

We will put on your armor and break the bow of steel
The sword of your spirit mightily, we will by unction wield
To you alone, Jehovah, every soul that lived will yield,
as with every devil, which is underneath your heel.

No heart will resist your glory, no knee will deny your throne
All tongues will confess your sovereignty, all life its creator know.
You are the everlasting—the only way to life
Your truth is all sustaining—you shall not be denied.

Reflect—Question—Ponder—Pray

Take time to mediate on these words and let the many things God is to us sink in.

From your personal experience, is there anything else you would add to this list?

_____

_____

_____

_____

_____

Can you think of a time when God has defended or protected you?

_____

_____

_____

_____

_____

This passage also alludes to our responsibilities: following God's instructions and commandments, and standing against evil and the things that are not of God. The majority of our society is made up of ideas, values, and beliefs that stand contrary to God's principles. What are the areas you struggle with the most (*e.g., it may be particular TV shows, song lyrics in certain music genres, partaking in criticism and gossip, indulging in excessive behaviors or lifestyles, drinking more than you should, and going clubbing just because everyone else does*)?

_____

_____

_____

_____

_____

_____

If you were banned from speaking about Christianity or wearing any Christian memorabilia, would people know you're a Christian from the way you behave?

_____

_____

_____

_____

This is not about condemnation; it's about being honest and self-reflecting. We need to be able to identify the areas where we struggle, come before the Lord in repentance, and ask him for the grace to change.

> *Father,*
>
> *I'm sorry for taking pleasure in things that don't bring you joy. I know it is a privilege being your child and I know you only want what's best for me. Lord, give me the strength and courage to let go of the things that don't edify me, and to release me from the indulgences and habits that have power over me. Create in me an appetite for things that are of you.*
>
> *In Jesus's name,*
>
> *Amen*

THE GREAT "I AM"

I'll pave the way through a grave
I'll take the keys of death away
I'll expose darkness with truth
I'll condemn the devil's abuse.

I'll open my flesh to bridge the gap
I'll bring the rights to heaven back
I'll heal every broken land
By being as silent as a lamb.

I'll be reviled and shamed
To crown you with my name
I'll be falsely accused
As a sacrifice for you.

I'm the offering—I'm the bread
I'm the wine—whose blood was shed
I'm the everlasting light
I'm the Word that came to life
I'm your judge and I'm your friend
On me you always can depend
I'm the shepherd of the sheep
I tell the stars when they can sleep
I'm who causes waves to stand
And sets up kings and rules all lands
I own every cattle on the hill
To me alone all bow and yield
I'm the well, the eternal spring
The living fountain of everything
I'm the Christ, the sacrificed
The one who died, to raise up life.

Wow, Jesus really did it all for us! Our everything depends on what he accomplished, because of what he was willing to lay down. It's comforting to know our hopes and dreams rest on the infallible rock of Christ. It also humbles us when we realize we can't make any of it happen by ourselves. The Bible tells us we don't even have the ability to add a single minute to our lives; it also goes on to say that if God is not in it, we build in vain.

Can you recognize areas of your life where you're at the steering wheel and in full control? What about relationships (*intimate, friendships, work*)? Are these areas you invite God into?

_____

_____

_____

_____

_____

As humans, from childhood and through education, we're continually empowered to make the best of ourselves and forge our own way. But in God's Kingdom, he asks us to humble ourselves: to be meek, to serve others, and to pray for those who spitefully use us. What aspects of Christian life do you find the most challenging?

_____

_____

_____

Can you name who Christ might be to you in those circumstances? (*e.g., in situations at work, where people are being derogatory about others or gossiping, it can feel uncomfortable. Here, Christ becomes my confidence and courage to politely excuse myself and walk away*).

_____

_____

_____

_____

CREATION SPEAKS

Mighty, awesome, loving God
Moving, creating, incredible God
God of wonder and God of light
God of splendor and awesome might
God of structures, you clothed with skin
God of breathing and invisible things
God of moonlight, sun, and stars
God of color—how wondrous you are!
God of fragrance, scents, and smells
God of heaven, earth, and hell
All who dwell do well to know
From this earth to one must go
Through the gate of Christ is life—
or through their flesh in sin to die.

Reflect—Question—Ponder—Pray

Isn't it incredible that God chose how many hairs to put on your head? He chose your height and the tone of your voice. He decided the exact length between your elbow and wrist. The Bible says he named all the stars, and he calls them out one by one. How amazing is that! God is purposely intentional and the beauty of his creative power is permanently on display.

The Bible says that every good and perfect gift comes from God. Do you find it easy to recognize and acknowledge that he is the source of all the things you take pleasure in? Take the time to list some of them here, and let the Lord know how grateful you are for them.

The first book of Genesis tells us, that when God made us, he called us "very good." However, it's very easy to look around, via society, the media, the Internet, and TV, and feel like we don't measure up. But of all the beautiful things in nature, God names us his very best.

What do you think are the main influences that determine how you feel about yourself?

_____

_____

_____

_____

_____

What barriers are stopping you from accepting and loving you, as you currently are?

_____

_____

_____

_____

_____

What steps can you take to minimize your exposure to negative influences? How will you spend more time finding out who God says you are?

Transfiguring

There's fruit from our labors in your earth
Upon salvation you lifted the curse
Seed for the sower and bread to the same
Your righteous are never put to shame
No one who takes up the name above names
Can ever, in any format, be the same
In a proclamation of glory they can now be found
Coz at that name of Jesus all bow down
All are blown away
The "I AM" silences every accusation and blame
Reduces to rubble every wicked way
Shatters every falsehood and claim
Breaks every chain
Every weapon starts to decay
Every plot goes up in flames
You're the ancient of days
Creation does what you say
You say stand on my promises
And see my mighty arm displayed
You say get to know me by reading my ways
That book of life is our legal claim
Blood bought when the lamb was slain
Adopted and transported by Christ's fame
Pardoned and renamed
Holy Spirit now flowing through our veins
Brothers and sisters, we will never be the same
Let heart, mind, and spirit God's name proclaim
Hallelujah, we will never be the same
Hallelujah, in Christ we're eternally changed!

Reflect—Question—Ponder—Pray

The Bible tells us that Jesus took captivity captive. This means that everything that previously held us, confined us, and limited us was utterly destroyed. Without fully understanding what Christ's victory achieved for us, it's easy to remain captive to cycles of doubt, fear, addiction, and failure.

However, as soon as we lay claim to the fact that the name of Jesus subdues and has power over every negative emotion, situation, circumstance, and thought, we step into alignment with God just by believing what he has said, and everything that kept us bound is broken off.

List the areas of your life where you feel pushed aside or hemmed in.

_____

_____

_____

_____

You can use your own words or follow this simple prayer.

> Lord,
> I lay these areas where I feel restricted and confined before you, and I ask you by the power of Jesus's name to release me from every confinement and restriction in my life. Lord, your Word says that if I know the truth, the truth will set me free. Fill me with your truth so that I may live the liberated life Jesus died to give me, and stay liberated.
> In Jesus's name,
> Amen

CHECKMATE

O death, where is your sting?
The ancient graves no longer call you king
The souls of men no longer walk in chains
Captivity from your fame has been erased.

O Death, your hold was slain
We're now upheld by the name above names
Like an eagle we soar and fly—there's no more darkness to
blacken our skies
The name of Jesus has emblazoned our lives!

Your marks and scars have been washed away
We looked you in the eyes, death, and roared Christ's name
We walked away . . . there was nothing left to say
You were swallowed up by Christ's empty grave.

Your grave clothes no longer cling to our backs
We also gave your shame and misery back
Your ashes near us cannot be found
We've been beautified with our savior's crown.

His victory our eternal win
Pardoned and absolved from every sin
Triumphant in his hands from above
Fearless in our savior's love
We tremble only at your majesty
Our only defeat is not to bow our knees
In awe of your magnificent supremacy.

If the ultimate contester of our human existence—death—could not hold Jesus back, and the very same Jesus now lives in you, realistically, what can ever get in your way? The Bible tells us that the devil is the father of lies. He's constantly trying to make us believe that our situation or problem is bigger than our God, or, even worse, that God isn't interested in our situation because we got ourselves into the mess in the first place.

These are two of the most prolific lies of the devil, and he uses them to breed death. He wants to kill our relationship with our loving Father in heaven.

Before you were even born, God knew every mistake and sin you would commit. He knew every wrong decision you would take, how many times you would choose not to forgive, and how many times you would purposely disobey him because you wanted your own way. He knew all this and yet he still chose to pursue you and make you part of his family!

If God wanted perfection, he would have created perfect human beings, or given us no choice or will of our own. But he gave us all these things because he desires a relationship with us and he wants us to learn to trust him.

God's love is bigger than your mistakes, and his mercy is mightier than your worse sin. So next time negativity, doubt, condemnation, or shame tries to flood your thoughts and heart, call on the name of Jesus and ask him to fill you with the knowledge of the perfect victory he won for you.

Stay blessed,
Amen

To You Honor Is Due

Your throne room is a communal place
Where confession lets you in
And believing casts off every sin
Where grace lines the floor
And honoring you unlocks the door.

Your name is greatly to be feared
In fear and trembling it should be revered
It consumes every false thing as we draw near
It purges all the dross and takes away the tin
In the forge of your consuming fire, new life does begin.

You're the great refiner and purifier of all things
And into your jealous love, us children enter in
None can escape your processing of gold
Your ways, our Father, are proven from old.

Your presence is the most holy thing
It is more than folly to presumptuously enter in
To grieve your spirit is a most deadly thing
You named it the sin above everything
So even if your voice we have never heard
We must determine to live and walk by your Word.

Reflect—Question—Ponder—Pray

Whenever you feel separated from God, or if you've done something that makes you feel like you don't want to come into his presence, just know that although you may feel distant, he is ever near. His Word says he will never leave or forsake us.

Yes, God is perfectly holy and yes, he's righteous and just, which means that sometimes there are consequences when we totally miss the mark. But even in the depths of our worst, he's never further away than the words, "Hi, Lord."

He never turns a deaf ear, he never ignores us. In fact, the Bible tells us numerous times that he is jealous over us! It is always in his heart to restore us to truth, peace, and joy in his Holy Spirit.

When you feel you've messed up, what's your default mode of action?

_____

_____

_____

Are you comfortable with the knowledge that like any loving parent, God will reprove and correct us, in order to help us mature? What do you think is the source of your comfort or discomfort?

_____

_____

_____

_____

_____

Do you view repentance as something positive or negative? Why?

_____

_____

_____

_____

The power of repentance is that when we fall short, which all of us do on a daily basis, we have an advocate, Christ Jesus, whose blood speaks on our behalf in the heavens and says, "My blood paid for this." There may be some implications to our decisions here on earth, but in heaven there never will be. This is because through repentance we step into the power of Christ's sacrifice on Calvary, and that same sacrifice helps us to overcome the choices and decisions that leave us feeling disappointed and separated from God, in the first place.

Not By Might

WE ARE NOT CALLED to enforce God's kingdom and commandments. He's not a dictator—he deals with us through grace. He disciplines through love and brings us to repentance, not by condemning us or pointing out our wrongs, but by giving us the truth. When we're exposed to his truth and light, we are able to see our own errors and recognize when our motivations stem from places of hurt, ignorance, or doubt.

God never wants us to judge people, because he didn't pass judgement on us. Instead, he sent his son to die in our place, because he placed his relationship with us above all else. God mourned Adam and Eve's decision in the garden, but he gave free will and choice. He wasn't looking to create servants or slaves—he wanted us as friends.

When we judge others and harbor unforgiveness or brood on offenses, we are effectively saying that our thoughts, feelings, and experiences are more important than the mercy and blood of Christ.

The Bible is full of so many incredible promises. Where we make a small commitment, such as believing, then God does the rest. But when it comes to forgiveness, God says, to paraphrase, "I will show you forgiveness as you show others; the mercy you dish out is the same amount of mercy you'll receive."

And in the honesty of our hearts, we know this makes total sense. In Christ we've been forgiven for everything: every sin—past, present, and future—and every evil deed and wicked thought was tallied up and intentionally paid for by Christ. So in effect, how dare we not show mercy to another? How dare we hold another to the account of their wrong, when Christ was murdered on account of ours?

Like I mentioned, repentance is the most liberating thing in the world. It sets you free from the lies and horrible thoughts about yourself, others, and even God.

As you read this chapter, don't be afraid to ask God for help—that's what he's there for. Ask him if you're carrying any unresolved resentment, unforgiveness, offense, or bitterness. Nothing will bring him greater joy than to see you set free from other people's words and actions.

DID IT HURT YOU TO DIE FOR ME?

You said it hurt you more to be estranged
Sin, the fall, Adam and Eve—it all got in the way
A gulf of darkness, a wall of shame—dying for me was the only
way
A bodyguard takes a bullet . . . a lesser life, a smaller price
But you're the one that did it—and you're the Christ!
It's like sacrificing the wineskin for what's inside
The very nature of your substitution confounds the human mind
The greatest for little grains of sand
The majesty for the subjects of his land
Christ, I'll never understand . . .
I guess that's why you're God and I'm just a man.

Reflect—Question—Ponder—Pray

Sometimes the knowledge that every wrong, bad or poor decision
we make has already been paid for doesn't seem real. It can be hard
to process that we never have to be ashamed or afraid of condemnation, as God never accuses us.

The world we live in is not so forgiving. People are constantly
trying to remind us of how we used to be, or they try to use our
past to keep us in a place or at a level that they are comfortable
with.

The reason why people try to hold onto our past mistakes is
due to their own insecurities. When they see us progressing and
advancing, they are left with no excuse but to accept that where
they are in life is predominantly their choice.

This can be a hard and bitter pill for many to swallow; we live
in a culture of blaming everyone but ourselves. But self-reflection
and acknowledging our own contribution to any given situation is
the beginning of maturity and growth.

As Christians, Christ is calling us to maturity, because he knows the world needs people who will tolerate and love them (turn the other cheek) and not shut them out based on how they behave.

That's what Our Father does with us; he doesn't treat us according to our behavior. Instead, when he looks at us, he only sees the perfect blood of Christ—the blood that covers all our transgressions and mistakes. And we are commissioned to see the same, to view each other—even our offenders—as God views them. To view them as his creations, each fearfully, uniquely, and wonderfully made, and to view them in light of the mercy and forgiveness that we ourselves have received.

The Two Lanes Of Mercy

We were loved and plucked from sin
So how do we so quickly enter in—to showing no mercy when we
feel done in?
To not seeing others through their eyes—not seeing their failures
could be ours in disguise
Oh, Lord, you said not to judge what's in a brother's eyes—when
we are technically legally blind
There's no measure of sin—it's not the best ones that get in—we
all fell short, all our works came to naught
So how do we dare accuse others and say it's their fault?
You didn't die for revolt of flesh against flesh, but you died to end
the onslaught of death
Let's lay down our weapons of what we can see: our fight is
against spiritual forces and principalities
The fight is never between you and me!
Thank you, Lord, for revealing what the devil didn't want us to
see
We're not victims—we have the victory!
Heirs of salvation, we were resurrected to new life.
Your death buried those grave clothes of bitterness and strife.

Reflect—Question—Ponder—Pray

Why do you find it hard to forgive?

24

Do you feel forgiven and accepted by Christ, or do past and present mistakes still hang over you?

_____

_____

_____

Do you think experiences where you have not been shown tolerance or forgiveness have made it harder for you to show mercy and love?

_____

_____

_____

Offense is a tool of the enemy to keep people bound in bitterness, resentment, and strife. With this knowledge, how will you prepare your heart differently the next time someone offends or insults you?

_____

_____

_____

_____

_____

The Root Of Condemnation Is Pride

The root of all condemnation is pride
It's acting like someone else hasn't tried
It's like gorging yourself on self-inflating lies
It's like not using love to bring someone to the other side
It's like ignoring the compassion that was shown to your life.

Condemnation hates
It doesn't give mercy a place
It's never prepared to look the other way
To teach rather than to throw hate
To release . . . remembering that we all sin
Forgetting it was Jesus who forgot our mess and took us in
It's easy to blame—condemnation demands you pay
Instead of pouring the blood that washed our weaknesses away.

Condemnation is dark
It's the very hand tool of the devil's art
Trying to scrap the Holy Spirit's fresh start
Lying that your sin was bigger than Jesus's part
It's a spirit that will use any "friend"
Twisting truth for its satanic end
To malign, bully, and torment
Denying the blood
Denying God's true love.

Condemnation is jealous of God's love
Jealous that in our utter ruin, he still washed us in his blood
Your still carry us, elevating us in perfect love.

There's no penance to pay
No Hail Marys to say
Honestly, the blood of Jesus has paved the way
The only words we have to say
Are, "Forgive me, Father" and "Change my ways"

In God there is no hate
It's never too late
He's waiting to pluck out the thorns and heavy weights
To change our hurts and how we relate
To remove those internal obstacles that stand in our way
We never know how far our hearts are from his truth
That's why he's always calling and speaking to you
He doesn't have a negative word to say
Christ saying, "Forgive them" catered for every mistake
He says to sit at his table—not outside on a stool
Once you're in Christ nothing can ever disqualify you
Condemnation is the opposite of his truth
He died as a sacrifice for you—it's our greatest proof
Of the depth of his love and what he's willing to do!

Lord Jesus, we thank you,
Amen

Reflect—Question—Ponder—Pray

Condemnation really is about playing judge, jury, and executioner. When it's spelled out like this, it's pretty ugly, yet I am sure we can all relate to this passage. And also see how prideful, selfish, and inhumane condemning another person is.

If you feel there is someone in your life you have condemned and passed judgement on, take it to the Lord in prayer and ask him to forgive you, and also for the grace to forgive them from your heart, releasing yourself from every root of pride, resentment, hurt, and, bitterness.

Ask him to flush out all the toxic and negative emotions and replace them with his peace, tolerance, humility, and love.

In Jesus's name,
Amen

It Begins With Knowing How Weak I Am

Our most tender parts are unseen and out of them flows the
things of our hearts:
My thoughts, my being, my cares, my woes, make up the
expressions of a God-fearing soul.

My frame is as fragile as the trust whereupon I lean
It falters when resting on things that are seen
But when it's placed on that infallible rock and bows its knee to
the only God
When it is postured before the king of all kings and surrenders to
the creator of all and everything
Then dry bones replenish and my soul is knit, by the living Word
that both lived and was writ.

When on Christ alone a form is fed and gives its life to seek his
bread
Then ministering angels will water your head and peace will
cover you in your bed
When you fear our all-consuming God and know his arm does
not fall short
Then victory will overtake you like his bow and his arrow will
defeat your every foe
When worship satisfies your soul and to praise Jehovah makes
you whole
When you count it kindness to be known and receive reproofs
and his ways retold
Then fully brethren we testify, the Kingdom of God is clearly
nigh, our praises go up as we sing, and his glory invades our
everything.

Remember, we are allowed to—in fact, we are supposed to—tell God about all the things that bother and upset us. We're not supposed to keep all those things locked inside. He is the perfect person to trust with the depths and worries of our heart.

We can take comfort in knowing that he genuinely cares, plus he is also interested in moving us past our feelings of hurt. He is the only one who can administer the healing and strength we need to let go and move on.

Our heavenly Father loves it when we talk to him; he never sees it as us grumbling or moaning. In fact, he relishes that we trust him by pouring out our hearts to him first. It's a form of worship, as we're acknowledging him as our source, protector, and savior.

So next time you're feeling down, weary, or fragile, talk to him like you would a friend—he's waiting to hear from you!

HELP AND HOPE

Help us, Father, to think on right—to keep pure justice in our
sights
Let not our emotions contaminate truth
Let not our hurt rebuke reproofs
There's no satisfaction in seeing others in pain
Their moans and despair could never take ours away
So let us not be fools in the devil's games
He's the only enemy we should name and blame
It's not flesh we should address—it's never carnal things
It's the principalities and rulers, the evil that's unseen
Our weapons of warfare are also tolerance and love
We're all weak in flesh and we all will mess up
So strengthen us, Father, to focus and trust
And forgive all offenses—like you did with us.

Reflect—Question—Ponder—Pray

Be honest with yourself and list all the things that tend to offend
you, or make you feel frustrated or angry (*e.g., when others don't
acknowledge your efforts, when others are shown favoritism, or
when you're not thanked*).

_____

_____

_____

_____

_____

The Bible says that when we are weak in Christ we are strong, because his grace is sufficient. For each area listed above, ask God for the ability to recognize it as soon as it comes, and for the grace to overcome it.

REGARDLESS

It's wrong to be wronged
And regarded of no esteem
Your Word said we should show no man partiality
But they browse with disdain when looking at me
They cannot see your treasures of gold, deposited in me
Everybody just wants to follow after the riches they can see
Hungry for what's proclaimed, with no regard for the beauty of a
holy name
Conniving for what brings respect, no regard for the lowly, no
debts of regret
No mercy for those they've upset
A penny thrown to ease their own souls, a pat for their back, but
they never turn back
So easy to be cold, and dismiss . . .
Not knowing it's the glory of God you've missed.

Reflect—Question—Ponder—Pray

So what do we do when we've forgiven, and forgiven, and forgiven
some more, and yet we still don't get any respect; we're still not
treated any better or appropriately?

It can be exhausting when you're continually trying to do the
right thing without seeing any reward. In these cases, there is only
one thing we can do—cry out to God.

We must never take matters into our own hands; we must
never try to beat others at their own game or stoop to their tactics and cheap digs. Firstly, the Bible tells us that there is only one
judge, the Father, God of all heaven and earth. Only he has the
authority to judge, as only he has the power to save or destroy;
only he knows the thoughts and intentions of each heart. Secondly,
we serve a just and righteous God, who promises to avenge and

recompense us for every evil and injustice. It is our job to wait on him, obey him, and keep our hands clean!

When you feel you're being unjustly treated, what is your de-stress mechanism?

_____

_____

_____

_____

The Bible tells us in the Gospel of Luke, chapter 17, that throughout life, offense is guaranteed. (It also says woe to those who it comes by!) So, with this knowledge in mind, having a detox mechanism or routine in place is essential. We need a way of emptying out the wounding words and actions of others.

Start by listing the activities, songs, or places that help you reach a place of peace.

_____

_____

_____

_____

Keep this list in a handy place, such as your wallet, purse, or on a memo note on your phone.

For All Have Sinned
And Come Short Of The Glory Of God

I can no longer judge when beholding an image that is yours
It would fail me to not love—when it was for all sins you endured,
But I cannot think myself higher nor deem myself below,
I can only be what by fire and anointing you've bestowed.

I cannot harbor unforgiveness when you chose affliction by my
sins
It was my roots of bitterness that pierced your side, it was my hate
that denied a Christ
It was my greed that cast those blows and sought your garments
by a dice throw
It was my pride that spat and looked upon you with haughty eyes
And that crown of thorns mirrored all that I despised.

It was my neglect of holy things and my lust for the ungodly,
accursed, and unclean
That built that cross, that betrayed, that took the silver and looked
away,
That picked that stone, and cheated the poor, and looked for
men's praises with no regard for your law
I was that whitewashed tomb without, which fasted so in the
market I could lament out loud
That washed my hands but not my heart, that sort to gain, but not
from sin depart
I was that judge and jury and crowd—the lukewarm who at first
cried out, "Hosanna, blessed are you, oh king," and then with the
same breath, "Crucify him!"

So how could I ever judge? Or think myself more clean . . .
Did not Christ die for all? Was it not grace that redeemed?
Did not all fall short? Were not all our deeds stained red?
Did not all our faults deserve death? Was it not Christ who died
instead?

If God found fit to forget and put all my iniquities away,
If El Elyon found you righteous then in love I'll do the same

So I will no longer judge when beholding an image that is yours
In remembrance I will love—for it was all our sins you endured.

Reflect—Question—Ponder—Pray

We're ending this chapter with our position in Christ, when it comes to forgiveness. We can't live a hypocritical life; we must show and act out the mercy we have received.

Amen and stay blessed

Unguarded

THIS ISN'T AN EASY chapter, as it mirrors all the ways our eyes, hearts, minds, and emotions can be contaminated when we don't guard what we expose ourselves to.

Simple things such as social media, magazines, and TV can fill us with opinions and ideologies that are totally contrary to the ways of God.

We have to be intentional with what we consume. We know from the Parable of the Good Seed that the Word of God can take root in our hearts, and hopefully go on to produce a one-hundred-fold harvest. However, the reverse is also true, meaning words of the flesh, of pride, from selfish ambitions, and from the devil can also sink into the soil of our hearts and desires, bringing forth "bad" fruit.

It is my hope that as you progress through this chapter, you'll be able to acknowledge and accept where you've fallen prey to such thoughts, attitudes, and opinions. This is the first step and we should all take comfort in knowing that God reveals things to redeem and restore us. Hearing us confess our sins doesn't make God feel good. What makes him jump for joy is when we're freed from the lies and deceptions that cause us to get tangled up in such nonsense in the first place.

Take the time to write down any traits or issues you recognize and take them to the Lord in prayer, asking him to remove any propensities and appetites you have for the things that are not of him. Ask him to reveal to you areas or habits that are exposing you to ideas that plant ungodly seeds. Finally, ask him to show you how to guard your heart, mind, emotions, and spirit, and to be mindful over what you allow your eyes and ears to consume.

If you have children, you can also ask the Lord to help you do the same for them.

Amen

Pandemonium

Declare whose allegiance you pledge, whose mark or emblem
you'll wear on your head.
I just want to be accepted, I just want to be liked, without lying to
myself and the truth having to hide.
Trying so hard to conform and fit in, with their rules and their
fashions about what's good and what's in! What I should study,
what I should read, the labels to dress in, and where to be seen.
Who makes these lists anyway? Of course, we're not all built the
same. So why are they trying to mold us that way? I guess that's
how the corporates get paid.
We're branded cattle, hooked on TV and falsified images in
magazines, food-like substances are what we're fed; Chihuahuas
in little bags are better nourished and better kept. Increased
spending, waists extending, proteins to shake away the guilt,
caffeine to suppress all ills. Health foods condemn the underpaid,
sugar in crisps lead the best efforts astray. Vitamins in every
lotion and cream—but in our food they can't be seen.
Yoga incarcerated a generation, action turned to sedation. You
can't hum your problems away, or do fancy stretches whilst the
morals of life decay. Vision boards, momentum stalled, sellotape
instead of having your say, decorating your walls instead of
tearing down hate. Wanting to be *The Apprentice* but possessing
no appreciation for work, no appetite for process, no hunger for
real success. Looking for the social steroid instead, where you can
get upgraded for how you dress or for flashing flesh.
Conversation went to the grave as virtual reality took its
place; swipe right to contact for a night, winks and drinks to
manipulate. Dating's changed—apparently you get them by
"playing the game." Box sets became assets in divorce, a lack of
a monogamy emoji to communicate rules! Bartenders see more
fathers than kids, mothers more concerned with the life they have
missed. The emotionally starved on TV, the socially inept spam
our news feeds, pictures for every blink, hungry for every like

and wink, addicted to that notification tone. Deaf to facts, just
psychologically indebted to those whoever respond's back.

No wonder online became infectious as insecurities went viral.
But wait . . . get a snack . . . then our "Top ten tips to get your life
back!"

Reflect—Question—Ponder—Pray

Does any of this sound familiar?

_____

_____

_____

Have you ever found yourself caught up in the ideas and trends of
others?

_____

_____

_____

Do you think you're easily influenced by what you hear and see
around you? Do the issues of other people or society easily become
yours?

_____

_____

The whole point of the social rhetoric and pressure to conform is to drown out our own original thoughts and identities. It's very easy to adopt a fashion or style, or to pick up gadgets because they reflect a certain status or lifestyle. Often we don't even question whether any of this suits us, or if we really like what we're consuming. We just accept what we're told is good for us, or we assume others (the richer, prettier, more successful, and more handsome) know better than us.

Someone having a platform, stage, or microphone doesn't make them more qualified or knowledgeable than you! Next time, take time to pause and ask why you're really doing something. You can also ask the Holy Spirit to help guide you, and to reveal the real source of your motivations. We too often buy into other people's ideals, instead of our own.

Beating Against The Wind

Now everything's offense or defense, get enraged, and have
your say, print that shirt and raise a plaque, or go rioting in
propaganda's hat.
Every voice is braying for a place, screaming for vengeance in the
government's face. We're all being urged to take a stake, voting to
expel all that we hate, hoping to preserve what's already decayed.
Afraid to admit we only have ourselves to blame. Ignorance can
no longer be feigned. Indifference has barraged our space, but
when staring at a grave of conceit, I guess it's easier to point at
you than at me.
So it's you, us, or them—it's a war, it's a fight, declare your
position, who has ever wronged your right? Who won't bow and
do what you do, and won't promote yours as the only truth? Who
won't fall in line and pave your way? Who won't surrender their
opinion and give ear to what you say?

It's madness, I don't want the strife, because they don't like how
you look, what you like. They don't like your surname or skin,
they don't like the stones in your wedding ring. Pay you less
because you wear a dress, says it's your fault if your skirt is too
short. Justice only if you can pay, else be a good girl and look the
other way.

So now integrity keeps you out of the room, and its "favors" that
promotes you through. With money the new currency of truth,
nepotism created a solid roof. Profit the one with the whip, your
balance sheet determines if you should die or live. Sustainability
got locked away and corporate sponsorship took her place.

All this . . . we let have its way, because everyone wanted their
own say.

Reflect—Question—Ponder—Pray

The Bible speaks mightily about the power of unity; how one person can put one thousand enemies to flight, but how two can cause ten thousand to flee! Those are amazing numbers; they show that the power of agreement follows God's principles of multiplication. Genesis 11, the story of the Tower of Babel, tells us that because these people were all of one mind and had the same agenda, nothing was impossible for them. Wow, wow, wow. God said they would succeed in any endeavor because they were all in agreement.

Imagine if we, all the many different members of Christ's body, came together in agreement, to act as the salt and light to the world, as Christ commanded us, instead of being fractured by denominations and over doctrines, rules, and varying interpretations. If all us Christians could lay aside differences and agree, the world we live in would be a very different place. Nations and people would be subdued and convicted, recognizing the power of Christ in our unity.

But we live in a society, and we have governments and policies that seek to further fracture and divide. Everyone likes to cast blame or throw hate, saying things like: "Yeah, it's entirely their fault"/"They're stealing all our jobs"/"They're all terrorists"/"It's her fault for dressing like that"/"It's the teachers, they're not teaching our kids right," and so on.

The world has completely perverted the word individualism; they've used it to encourage selfish ambitions and as an excuse to vocally abuse those you hate. However, true individualism is about recognizing that everybody is unique, and that everybody should have an opportunity to be heard and the freedom to express their truth. Our truth should never sound like hate or blame, it's simply expressing or articulating what something means to us or how it makes us feel.

Every sort of division or strife comes from the enemy. When we're divided or when everyone is out for themselves, we become ineffective at standing against the forces of injustice and darkness.

The greatest power you have in society and your strongest currency are the choices you make and the actions they result in. Corporations, media, influencers, advertisers, brands, marketers, and the devil are all scheming, pressurizing, and using every form of tactical manipulation to control your choices. As Christians, we are called to choose unity, reconciliation, and peace, while never contributing to the divide.

What are your thoughts on the state of division in your nation and communities? How can you be an agent of change?

_____

_____

_____

_____

_____

God, You Have To Be Up There

Who could scarce believe in such a love? Who would dare trust
in the heavens above? But who could deny a hungry heart, and to
find a fit and know one's part? If all that is seen is corruption and
decay, but in an unseen soul lies hopes for grander days. Then
surely in the depths of despair, on those lonely nights when no
one else cares, and in those hollow moments of, "Who's out there?
Does anyone see? Will anyone want to know the real me?"

To a diary I write of a thousand fears, and to my pillow I sow
an ocean of tears. The night robs me of my self-esteem, when I
worry about how I will be judged and perceived. In the morning,
I shower with my head on the wall, as I imagine I was skinnier
and six-feet tall; with a powerful job and beautiful clothes, and a
doting husband who writes love notes.

But instead I buy those silly magazines, which only makes me
hate a little bit more of me. My friends, I love them, they are
truly great, but when will we all move past playing dress-up, like
when we were eight? We're not even honest, apparently it's not
allowed. Us grownups have grown cold as we've grown proud. I
know you're as anxious as me; it's an obvious sign language that
everyone sees, a raging disability to which we all concede. So
how can I share my bitterness of disbelief with this life, when
we're all in the same boat and we're all left out to dry? Stranded to
ponder a world of strife, even worried about the youths outside.
Concerned if we'll get enough pay, and credit card bills for stuff
thrown away. Striving to have it all, climbing up ladders, for
something else to crumble or fall. Consuming, consuming, but
never, ever feeling full.
Wondering, what was the point of all this—what was the point of
this all?

Does any of this resonate with you?

_____

_____

_____

_____

Do you ever feel lonely or isolated in your fears and concerns about life?

_____

_____

_____

As a Christian, do you ever feel pressured to have it all together?

_____

_____

_____

_____

_____

It's very easy to portray a lifestyle or identity we're not actually living. However, you can relax, Christ is not asking us to live as the image of his perfection to the world, nor is he asking us to be his defender.

He can do that all by himself—he doesn't need our help or for people to stick up for him.

What he's calling us to is a life of authenticity, where we can be free and honest enough to express our true thoughts, where we don't feel the need to hide away our anxieties or concerns because Christians are not supposed to act that way or to have those issues. Us Christians are not immune to the challenges and suffering that come with being human. The difference is we have a wonderful savior to call upon—he'll step into our situation and give us the grace and courage we need to overcome things with joy. He'll also rescue us when we are in danger and heal us from the things that have scarred, wounded, and numbed our emotions.

So never be afraid to express even your disappointments and frustrations with the Christian life. When you pour yourself out to God, he's guaranteed to move on your behalf!

INFECTIOUS IDEOLOGIES

So, I'm watching reality TV and obviously I don't believe anything I see, but somehow it gets on the inside of me and I kinda start thinking I should apply and then become completely dissatisfied with my life. I seem so boring compared to what I've seen; I should have been on *The Real Housewives* on TV, instead of here in a onesie on my settee, with a mountain of debt from a degree and a fella I have to beg for a mug of tea. They have perfect waists and bums, nips and tucks in Hollywood sun, glossy skin and flowing hair, and every guy stops and stares. They're on the cover of magazines, babies then bikini DVDs. Ah, that seems the life for me. I'd objectify myself for TV, bare my flesh, flash my gems, show what only my husband used to see, for bundles of cash in magazines, hoping he doesn't cheat publicly and openly humiliate me. But then they say all men cheat and it's better to cry in a limousine! Or, better yet, get one of those old, rich guys, the ones that have more money left in them than life . . .

Reflect—Question—Ponder—Pray

It's so easy to become dissatisfied with our life, and to grumble about the things we should be grateful for. This is the real evil of comparison; it robs and blinds us to the truth, blessings, and abundance we possess. It causes us to look with disdain upon the things we begged and prayed to God for.

How do the things you see on TV or on social media make you feel about your own life? Do you think they alter how you perceive what's around you?

_____

_____

What areas of your life do you compare with others the most? Why do you think that is?

_____

_____

_____

_____

The Bible tells us in 1st Corinthians 10 that we're foolish if we compare ourselves with others. And when we think about it, that scripture makes sense; comparison truly is a double-edged sword. Comparing ourselves to others and faring positively can cause us to look down on others, allowing pride to seep in. Conversely, not measuring up can demotivate and demoralize us, in some cases leading to depression.

God only made one of us—we're all totally unique. Only God has the blueprint for your life. So nobody else is going to be able to tell you how to live it or what it should look like.

Read Psalm 139

It's a very powerful scripture and worth meditating on. Verse 10 tells you that God has already written down every single one of your days, and every moment of your existence. Take the time in prayer to ask the Lord to reveal all the things he wrote about you.

What Are We Breathing In?

Whitewashed—yet petrified within
No glamour can hide the stench of decay and sin
Too proud to repent, not bold enough to look inside
Not knowing your stubbornness is denying the power of Christ
Your stubbornness is denying you your access to life.

Boasting out loud . . . but not confessing you're proud
The words you won't speak are the keys to being freed
Sinful, shameless man that I am—
It's impossible that before such a holy God I could ever stand
Strip me of self, of flesh, and of sin
For thinking I'm the power, I make the things in my life end and
begin
Not knowing I'm suffocating my soul—
when the things of this world I refuse to let go
Not knowing I'm suffocating my soul—
when I think material wealth will make me whole
Not knowing I'm suffocating my soul—
when the words that I speak, only death they do reap
Not knowing I'm suffocating my soul—
and your Word says it's more precious than rubies and gold
What does it profit a man to gain all he desires—
yet lose the only thing that a holy God requires?

Reflect—Question—Ponder—Pray

It's a sad thing when jealousy creeps into our hearts. This happens to all of us at one time or another. It's often very subtle and not the green-eyed monster we're used to seeing on TV. It often seeps in because we're resentful of our Christian life. We see non-Christians and even other Christians having what looks like so much fun, with things coming so easily to them. And that makes us question our efforts of prayer, fasting, and self-discipline. We often do not realize that we're slowly growing cold-hearted to God and becoming envious of simple, frivolous living.

Read Psalm 73

Which parts stood out and what did you most identify with?

_____

_____

_____

_____

_____

_____

I believe the Lord wants to use this passage and psalm to call us into his presence to repent and be cleansed of the things that have crept into our thoughts and hearts.

Take this time to enter into his presence in prayer and allow yourself to be cleansed by his forgiveness.

In Jesus's name,

Amen

LUKEWARM

You give God two minutes of prayer
—you don't get what you want and moan he doesn't care
Two minutes spent on anything else in your life
—tell me would such attention make anything survive?
To me that seems like chronic neglect
—and to our savior, who above all commands all respect
You invest in one scripture
—devotionals are easier you say
—not knowing it's the words of the Bible that actually bring
change.

Worship, scripture, and prayer should be as routine to you as
breathing air
—it's not something you rush to when you're in despair
God seeks a relationship with his heirs:
—didn't you read that without maturity you're like a slave, still a
babe?
—why would he give you your inheritance if you're just gonna
squander it away?
To whom much is given, much is required the same
—what would two minutes spent on anything earn you these
days?
We have a savior whose words are guaranteed
—he said seek first my kingdom and everything else you will
receive.

Reflect—Question—Ponder—Pray

This is such a challenging passage, yet we can all admit that time
dedicated to God is the easiest thing to let slip. It's also easy to
justify to ourselves why we don't need to pray, study the Bible, or
even read it regularly.

However, the truth is that we will never walk in the fullness of our inheritance in Christ if we don't invest in the things of Christ—it's simple math.

What are the main things competing for the time you spend with God?

_____

_____

_____

_____

Where does the pressure to prioritize these above God, our creator, come from?

_____

_____

_____

_____

_____

Which of these four practices—prayer, studying the Bible, reading the Bible, worshipping God—will you commit to doing every day? What activity will you give up to accomplish this?

DELUSIONAL

Let's sprinkle on some Jesus while I'm at work
Say a little prayer (when there's nobody there)
Then back to being a yob and a spiritual slob
Sunday's packed up in my best clothes at home
It's a jungle out there—that loving people "soft stuff" has gotta go
Loving your enemies . . . jeez . . . you'll end up broke
It's an eye for an eye to survive the big smoke
Yeah, prayer, it's necessary—like when you get sick
But to get ahead in life, you've gotta be more slick
I'll pray in God's favor—I can handle the rest
What I really need is his promises without all the stress
I'm sure he'll understand . . .
I mean, the world has really changed since he was a man.

Reflect—Question—Ponder—Pray

We live in a world where it's a weakness to show the qualities of Christ; where if you show compassion and kindness, you're called foolish or gullible; where you're told that you're being ripped off if you help charities or homeless strangers on the street.

"You are what you eat" is a famous expression, and it's true of the words and options we take in. If we don't guard ourselves and feed on the right things, then self-serving and self-preserving principles will start to eat away at our tolerance, kindness, and love. Even worse, one bad experience can leave us thinking that church stuff is just for inside church!

However, leaning on our own strength, and using our own tactics and devices is a symptom of the world having crept in. In the Gospels, we read that we should seek first the kingdom of God's righteousness, and that everything else we require will be added. We don't have to compete for promotion or selection when we have Christ, knowing that following his will can only work out for our good.

God uses situations and challenges to help us mature and to build our resolve and faith. The places he wants to send us into won't always readily accept us. You can only be a light where there is darkness. So to help us be effective agents of change for his kingdom, he'll put us in situations where we learn to trust and depend on him.

In such places, we can't compromise our faith or integrity. We have to be secure in our identity as a child of God, one that outwardly lives their Christianity and doesn't just talk about it.

Ask the Lord to reveal any areas of your life where you've compromised your God-given identity in order to fit in.

_____

_____

_____

_____

_____

What are the practical steps you can take to better guard your heart and mind?

_____

_____

_____

_____

Let's pray:

Lord,

I'm sorry for every time I've let the words and opinions of others come before what you say about me. I'm sorry for all the ways I've chased after the things of the world instead of seeking first your kingdom of righteousness. Lord, strengthen me in those areas where I am weak, and teach me to guard your principles and truths.

In Jesus's name,

Amen

Dear Santa, I Mean Jesus

I want success and a high salary—without the stress or work
I want a loving family—with no compromise or hurt
I want perfection from others—without improving myself
I want my opinion to always matter above everybody else.

Reflect—Question—Ponder—Pray

Wow, how unrealistic! I mean, surely none of us are like that??!

The reality is that most of us make daily demands like these to God in prayer. We want everything he has to offer: every promise, every blessing, but without any of the conditions or work. You'll notice that every significant person in the Bible went through serious processing before stepping into their promise or prophecy.

God desires to give us most of the things we're asking for, but he desires more that we have the maturity, humility, and character to sustain and retain them.

God is about showcasing his glory in our lives, so that others may come to know him. Our lives are his testimony.

If we don't have the maturity and spiritual discipline to handle what he gives us, according to his principles . . . then what is the point? It's the same way you wouldn't give a brand-new sports car to a 14-year-old; there is a process—a coming of age and a passing of a test—to get a driving license. And a lot of the time, it's the same for the things we ask for from God.

If you read about the lives of Moses, Joseph, and Mary, they didn't just step into divine moments and positions. They were processed and prepared for it. Just look at Mary. During the time of her life when she should have been celebrated (marriage, childbirth), she was hidden and on the run from those seeking her child's life. All this was part of the preparation for being the mother, the faithful steward, of Christ as a child.

So the next time you pray, understand that you're also asking God for the process and preparation that comes alongside what you are asking for.

Is the process and preparation that comes alongside prayer requests something you've ever given any thought or attention to before?

_____

_____

_____

_____

_____

THE WAR ON TALENT

Organizational, oppressive regime
It's hard to detect, often served with cups of tea
Boxing you in and tying your sleeves—dismissing the truth with
a simple, "Please"
"Please understand, we don't do it that way," or, "Our cultural
ingrains are too hard to change!"
Thanks for trying, your energy is great, but we're stuck in doing
what's completely out of date
Too blinded by oppression to see the organization's fate—too
scared to admit that they hate it that way
So they do what was done to them
They act the very same
Then that master of oppression keeps winning the game
Whilst all talents and ambitions slowly fade away.

Everybody needs change—but that means admitting you're
walking in chains
Instead their lying on their mat, waiting for a sympathetic pat on
the back.

Lying on their mat, yet blocking the gate
If they can't get through then they'll block others in the way
Intrepid anger pent up into rage, but too oppressed to display
So they act it out through repressive red tape
Through shouting, "No Way!" and by canceling agendas and
saying "Not Today!"
Saying, "Come back!" when they know it will be too late…
It's how they act out their hate—by blocking the way
And thus oppression stays, whilst joy and excellence dissipates
All having pity parties over cake
Whilst their destinies decay.

How are the attitudes around you limiting what God wants you to do in your life?

_____

_____

_____

_____

Do you ever find yourself giving in to the way things are and have always been?

_____

_____

_____

Ask the Lord to reveal to you areas where your Christian identity has been stifled or boxed in. By partnering with the Lord, what actions can you take to break loose from mediocracy and low expectations?

_____

_____

_____

_____

My House Will Be Called
A House Of Prayer

Pedophile priests and pastors on porn
Is it any wonder the world treats your namesake with scorn?
Alters of holiness have been turned to a stage
Performances now determine the collection plate's weight
Entertaining spirits replaced your holy ghost
Nobody's even realized in years you haven't spoke . . .
Too busy looking for scriptures for how not to be broke
Happy to carry every other generational burden and yoke
Offerings as investments—not giving to the lamb that was slain
Nothing sacrificial about trying to make yourself a name
Nothing sacrificial about trading on God's fame
Investment criteria—"He's gonna bless me now, I've declared and
decreed and hollered out loud"
Prayer shawls and tapes, vision boards and oils, fasting, seven
steps, and hashtagging it all
Fasting to gain—not knowing it's about giving yourself away
Saying to your maker, "Have it all your perfect way"
Praying to profit—not praying to stay saved
Don't you know in the Bible he turned those five virgins away . . .

Reflect—Question—Ponder—Pray

It's sad that even in church we can be exposed to things that are not
of God. However, the New Testament tells us we're to work out our
own salvation with fear and trembling. No church is responsible
for managing your relationship with God; we don't need human
mediators—that's the very thing Christ came to abolish.

It's our responsibility to keep ourselves aligned with God,
his principles, and his ways. That's why the Bible encourages us
to soak ourselves in the Word and to pray in the spirit (Epistle of
Jude), building ourselves up in the most holy faith. The church

is an important part of fellowship, discipleship, building relationships, contributing, and maturing in Christ. But it can never be a substitute for your own personal relationship with Christ.

The reason some of the things mentioned in this passage occur is because individuals in positions of power and authority have not guarded their hearts and minds from the things of the world and the wiles of the devil. They've become susceptible to all the things we've been addressing in the chapter; and once we've been infiltrated, it's easier for more serious and dangerous things to flood in.

Proverbs 4 tells you that the course of your life depends on how well you guard your heart, whilst Psalms 51 will equip you with the prayers to keep your heart pure before the Lord.

Read: Psalms 51 and Proverbs 4

What have you learnt?

_____

_____

_____

_____

_____

He Loves You

You go to work every day—you work and labor to get paid
You pay attention, you strive and try—you do your best to be
kinda nice
You spend more time on your garden or hair—for Jesus there's no
time to spare
Spouting out, "God doesn't care," when he calls you to talk you're
hardly there!
You can't complain that this life isn't fair—saying church agendas
are full of despair
When you're not willing in prayer to forbear—and speak to the
God that created your air
You prioritize putting him last—sitting in church like at the back
of the class
Saying, "He knows what you need"—so why should you get on
your knees?
It's a relationship our tender God seeks—and its distance from
him that's keeping you weak
He's not a magician to pull treats out of air; he tenderly created
you and numbered your hairs
He wrote all your days in his ancient book, and he is waiting for
you to come take a look . . .
He's calling you to be what he created you to be—so humble
yourself and fall on your knees

You changeth not, you're always the same
Generation to generation, in majesty and power you reign
Saving the captives, setting sons and daughters free
Bringing all the lost souls into your family
To every cry you turn your ear, and reach to cast away the fear
The undernourished you always feed—with spirit bread and milk
and meat
You clothe us in Christ's robes of red, and place your name upon
our heads

The mind of Christ does grace our thoughts, and through your
spirit we are taught
Illumination in our hearts, no longer living in the dark—
how wonderfully gracious you are . . .
Making your temple where once there were scars
Filling up our empty jars
Your glory in our vessels of clay
Dying for us and not throwing us away
How wonderfully gracious you are
No words could ever explain
You are holier than all your names
Irrational in your love
Your mercy is unfounded
Your passion without reason
Your concern indescribable
You are undeniably love
You wrote it in Christ's blood
When did a king ever die for slaves?
That's why you're crowned above all names.

Reflect—Question—Ponder—Pray

Take the time to reflect on this passage and write down, in all honesty, what Christ really means to you.

_____

_____

_____

_____

We know the Christian walk can be hard sometimes, but it's in those moments that we must draw near and not sink away.

It pains our Father to see us caught up and entangled in lies, with false misconceptions about who he is and who he made us to be.

Christ didn't die so that we could put a cross bumper sticker on our cars; he died to break every yoke and bondage of falsehood. He died to destroy the deceptions we innocently and ignorantly walked into. He died to dismantle the false economies and pipe-dreams the world has to offer. He died, sacrificed himself, and took our place so we could live an abundant life.

So if you're not living a life of liberty, firstly, don't despair—there is no condemnation for any in Christ. Just make a decision today to reconnect with God on a deeper level. Ask him for the grace to walk in the fullness of all he desires for you.

God's love for you is incredible. Being filled with ideas, dreams, and opinions that are not from him separates us from his best, and Christ died to give us that best.

Adoration

BEING AMAZED BY GOD—ADORING him, thinking about how incredible, intricate, and perfect his ways are—is worship to him.

Worship is not just singing—it's anything we do that is all about him. Worship, praises, thanksgiving, is the only time we ever give something back to God—everything else is him doing things for us!

In the last chapter, we spoke about the things that can seep in and contaminate our relationship with God. Worshipping and adoring him is one of the simplest ways of flushing those things out. When we worship God, whether it be in words or by action, we open up the heavens around us and the glory of God fills the very atmosphere.

Whenever we're in a bad mood, having negative thoughts or feeling heavy and overwhelmed, worship is guaranteed to shift us into a place of ease, peace, and understanding. Praising God fills us with his joy and Nehemiah 8 tells us the joy of the Lord is our strength. Praising God shuts down feelings of worry, anxiety, and doubt, and it elevates God to his rightful position as Lord over our all and everything.

Worshipping God allows us to lose ourselves in his majesty; it gives us perspective and confidence in his words, which say, "All things work together for our good," "We are more than conquerors", and, our "Father God is always in control!"

Whatever is your usual manner, before proceeding, take some time out to worship God and dwell in his awesome presence.

Amen

Living Waters

There is a stream that flows from your throne of grace
It starts from heaven's most holy place
Its crystal waters releases the soul
Its Calvary currents make the poor man whole
Our great Jehovah, on the waters blows—and for every wounded
place, there now springs hope.

There is a stream that flows from your throne of grace
It reaches into our deepest place
Cleansing into both marrow and bone, clearing out every secret
stumbling stone
Making our most delicate thoughts known and rinsing out all the
debris, so we're purely God's home.

There is a stream that flows from your throne of grace
The water was shed whilst you were in total disgrace
They poured from your side while you were greatly maligned
Those piercing waters flowed when you were upon our cross
Those piercing waters flowed when we were totally lost.

There is a stream that flows from your throne of grace
Its crystal waters reflect the purity of heaven's host
Its healing powers mirrors the perfection of the lamb
In it we are delivered, its depth humbles every man
In it we are delivered by Jesus Christ, we now can stand.

There is a stream that flows from your throne of grace
It starts from heaven's most holy place
Its crystal waters releases the soul
Its Calvary currents make the poor man whole.
Amen

Reflect—Question—Ponder—Pray

Reflections:

_____

_____

_____

_____

_____

_____

Your Gentle Power

Your victory was history—yet it's my future and present tense
There are no measures to your days—ages bow down to what you
say
Your death was my birth—your resurrection buried my curse
Kings and rulers to you bow down—you created the earth in
which they're found
Your majesty is my crown—it's within your name my life's now
found
Your authority summons clouds—at your rebuke the waves fall
down
Your blood broke deadly chains—your silence brought heaven's
fame
You were the silent, sinless lamb—now elevated to God's right
hand
Your name above every name—the foundation we now proclaim
The stumbling stone became our home—the servant king now
lives within.

Reflect—Question—Ponder—Pray

Many of us don't get the deep, rich sleep that God desires for us. Our night-seasons (sleep time) are often when God communicates with us the most, because we're literally, physically, emotionally, mentally, and psychologically still. The Bible tells us in the book of Job, and throughout the psalms, that our sleep is also the time the enemy tries to sow seeds in our hearts and minds. These can be seeds of doubt, lies, anxieties, and fears.

I really believe the Lord wants to release you into a deeper level of comfort in your sleep. You can repeat the following prayer, if this is something you desire:

Lord,

I commit my sleep, rest, and night-seasons into your hands. I lay claim on your Word, which tells me my sleep will be sweet, and that it is you alone that causes me to lie down and sleep in peace. Lord, I cover my dwelling place, home, plus all of my physical and spiritual senses, with the blood of Jesus. Lord, in your power, shut down everything that is not of you and let me only hear your voice and dream your dreams whilst I sleep.

In Jesus's name,
Amen

It Starts With Who You Are

The Lord came riding on the winds, heavenly Hosanna's extended
like wings
With deception underfoot, he crowned every slave and bade
them to call on the name above names
With mercy he ruined the desolate place, and planted his people
in the soil of his grace
Destruction and debt and bondage and waste—fear, and
depression, he banished away
Sin soaked in shame, in corruption and guilt, he annulled with
his blood and condemned with his heel.

Oh, what manner of power is this, that in the death of a savior,
through a deceptive kiss, man could be restored to the image of
his?
In what glory, of what mind, could deep mysteries of love be so
reconciled? The creator would step into the dust of mankind,
transform the dirt, and rekindle God's life.

Reflect—Question—Ponder—Pray

Do you ever feel unworthy?

_____

_____

_____

_____

_____

Unworthiness can often stem from the hurtful words of others, or from the lies and condemnation of the devil. God counted you as his most precious prize—he didn't want us to live life without knowing how important we are to him.

If you're feeling any of the emotions in the first paragraph (fear, depression, guilt, etc.) know that these are not from God. He never points the finger, and he never tells you what you did was wrong for the sake of showing how bad you are. God never, ever criticizes us!

Worshipping God is one of the most powerful privileges we have. When we worship God, heaven takes over and invades everything to do with us, and everything around us.

So, when you're feeling heavy, flooded with negative emotion, or like you're under attack, put on some worship music and ask God to let his spirit, our Prince of Peace, take control.

Amen

THE AIR I BREATHE

How could I not be swept up in wonder
In the raiment of your love—when your heart is so very tender?
And showers me from above.
How could I not be astonished
At the beauty of your grace, which announces to me daily,
"You are blessed and you are saved"?
How could I not be ecstatic
That you're my favor-ruling judge—when what you decree is
established
In the earth from heaven above!
How could I not be expectant
When you own everything I see—and the very breath that
created Eden
Also created me!

Reflect—Question—Ponder—Pray

Can you think of any moments or testimonies that really made you
feel loved by God?

_____

_____

_____

_____

_____

Is it easy for you to accept Christ's love, and that he died and gave it all for you?

_____

_____

_____

_____

Write down what you think hinders you from believing in Christ's goodness towards you, and release these things to him in prayer.

_____

_____

_____

_____

_____

Adoration

I wanted to write you a letter from my heart—I want to express
how glorious you are.
But mere words fail me when thinking of your grace, so how can
my words compare to what you say?
So I'll sing you a love song with my life—a cascade of praise
poured out page by page.
Each day reflecting what you've written and said—my daily
thoughts as special notes.
Let my adoration be melodious to hear, and my obedience as
cymbals in your ear.
Let my love for others sound like a harp, and my faith a worship
that makes sin depart.
Let your laws play the chords of my heart, and when I walk in
your ways let tambourines play.
And when there is no sound, let it be because I'm kneeling down.
Let my silence only in you be found, and everywhere else declare
you out loud.

Reflect—Question—Ponder—Pray

I'm sure you've heard people say that prayer is a two-way conversation. After we've said our bit, we're supposed to wait to let God
speak. I know that can seem really odd, even uncomfortable, but
the truth is that God desires to commune with us above everything
else. He is constantly reaching out to us in so many ways.

Some people hear God audibly, some through dreams, visions,
thoughts, or a feeling. Some perceive him through circumstance,
the Bible, nature, or via other people. How do you feel God speaks
to you?

_____

_____

_____

_____

Is this something you want more of, or do you have any concerns in this area?

_____

_____

_____

_____

I often ask the Lord to give me confidence in what I hear from him, as well as the assurance that he won't intentionally let me get it wrong. I know God is not going to allow me to run off in the wrong direction and, when it all ends in a mess, say, "You heard wrong, that wasn't me." God is not like that; he wants us to know and trust his voice. Keep these truths in your thoughts and heart, and invite him to speak to you more.

By His Grace, For His Glory

By your grace, I bow down and say you are king
By your grace, I confess my everything
By your grace, I dare to behold such truth
By your grace, your fire my heart reproves
By your grace, my ears wanton for thy Word
By your grace, my knees fall to your earth
By your grace, you reveal intelligent things
By your grace, you lead me before earth's kings
By your grace, my tongue doth repeat thine heart
By your grace, your kingdom comes and evil departs
By your grace, your glory doth impart:
One Lord, one king, one spirit, one heart.

Reflect—Question—Ponder—Pray

Agreeing with God is the most powerful action we can ever take in life. In Psalm 2, the Bible tells us that if we asked, God would give us nations and the whole earth as a possession. Wow! Agreeing with God means believing what he promises in the Bible, praying these promises back to him, and then acting in accordance with those promises.

Can you think of a time when you've asked something of the Lord, then a short while later taken actions or decisions in the complete opposite direction (*e.g., asked God for a financial provision, but then taken out a loan*)?

_____

_____

_____

_____

God's ways and thoughts are so far above ours that when he talks, we often dismiss it because his instructions don't sound like what we want to hear.

Ask the Lord to forgive you for all the times you've dismissed his voice. Ask him to open your ears and heart to receive from him. Ask him for the faith to believe what he says and the grace to follow every instruction.

In Jesus's name,

Amen

Unfathomable

What can I say?
No one can know your ways
Incredible are your thoughts—incomprehensible your routes
There's really nothing that any human being can say
We can only pray your will and see it all displayed
Our logic has the strength of ants—against what you know to do
We could never piece it all together—so intricate and precise are
you
Our minds are like water in your hands—they run loose
That's why it's only your wisdom that understands and can recoup
So we just take faith in all that we do—knowing we're prayerfully
led by you
Not seeking to uncover some curious truths—
Just knowing you're righteous in all that you do.

Reflect—Question—Ponder—Pray

Which areas of life do you find most difficult to release over to
God?

_____

_____

_____

_____

_____

Why do you think you find it so hard to trust him?

_____

_____

_____

Do you think poor experiences with other people have negatively contributed to how you view a relationship with God?

_____

_____

_____

_____

We have a good, good Father; ask him to help you trust him completely and fully.
> *In Jesus's name,*
> *Amen*

The Mental Arithmetic Of Being Saved

THIS IS THE PART where most of us struggle. Where our memories of past experiences constantly wrestle with the notion of grace and a completely new identity in Christ.

It can feel like you're out of control and often out of your mind, as you try to marry everything you've heard in church with your own understanding of the Bible and your feelings about Christ's love.

We read a lot in the book of Romans about leaving behind the old man and the lusts of the world, and putting on our new identity and personhood in Christ. We hear about no longer being led by our carnal nature and the lies of the enemy, and being fully spirit-led instead. This doesn't happen overnight; it's a journey of seeking God's truth and trusting his processes.

We often forget that before we truly started a relationship with Christ (which can occur a long time after we accept him), we were our own free agents. We had preferences, habits, likes, dislikes, choices, and opinions. These were totally our own to use and to some extent we were largely happy with them. When we met Christ and started to recognize the quality of our internal emotions and thought-life, our identity, even our character and behavior, was way below God's best for us. Literally, all hell broke loose. The devil wants to keep us as ineffective, lukewarm Christians, and our own fleshy thoughts and desires want to keep up with the status quo. In the midst of all that is our transformed spirit man, who is crying out to God to be unconfined and set free from all the internal and external pressures of society, our minds, and our life.

The person we've always known is hard to let go of, but rest assured there is so much more in store—wonders you could not even fathom!

If, whilst reading this chapter, you recognize that you're in this phase, first of all there is hope, so don't give up. You're not going crazy, you're simply being renewed by the love of God. I hope the words here will show you that you are not alone. Your breakthrough is guaranteed, so keep on hoping and holding onto that perfect love of Christ—his words and promises never fail.

God is simply purifying us so we have the clarity and understanding to see what is of him, what comes from the desires of our flesh, and what comes from the devil. When we can see the full picture we can make informed, spirit-led choices and live the life God promised in his Word.

This chapter is an opportunity to be honest with yourself, to applaud how far you've come, but also to be focused and determined to reach your expected end.

You're in my prayers!

Hopelessly Entangled

In the depths of my mind, please, Lord, make your home
In those hidden parts where no one else knows
Where the chaos and jungle of distractions grow
It's where I'm hit by the arrows of the many bows
It's from the depths of my mind that the poisons flow
Lord, it's where I need you most
Lord, it must be ruled by your holy ghost
Lord Jehovah, Lord, king of heaven's host
Enter in the thickets and thorns and tear up the briers and beasts
with their horns
Level the plain, make the paths straight, and clear up the
emotions of bitterness and hate
Redress regret and failure and shame—uproot unforgiveness and
passing on blame
I don't want to live this way—it's the accuser of the brethren
pouring out hate
Lord, I don't want to be a mouthpiece in his game—I don't want
my finger used to defame
Oh, Lord, it doesn't even make sense—he just incites different
targets of continued offense
God, I'm breaking free—I know it starts with asking you to
rescue me
Forgive me, Father, for the part I've played in allowing evil to
cloud my mind, to invade my heart, to displace what I truly know
is good and right
To be enticed and to be drunk on hate—forgive me, Father, for all
these ways
Rescue me, Father, in your love and might—rescue what happens
in my mind at night
Strengthen me, Father, in your love for the fight—to always think
on what I know is right, to think on those things which are good
in your sight.
Amen

Many of us feel this way, think this way, and have hated this way. It's horrible; such thoughts come on so strong and can seem so plausible, often feeding off our own insecurities and hurts.

It's person after person, issue after issue, and offense after offense. This is the easiest way to recognize that the enemy is at work—when everyone's doing these things but we ourselves have no blame of fault in it.

The Bible tells us the devil is the "accuser of the brethren." So even if we have been legitimately offended, God gives us the grace to forgive and move on. This is simply so that nobody's words or actions can have any power over us in our minds or hearts.

Being drunk on hate is a very horrible place to be, but it's also a place that—with Christ's help—we can be permanently free from. Come before him in repentance today and ask him for forgiveness for every time you've let hate, anger, bitterness, and resentment, etc., have a place in your heart and thoughts. Ask him, in his mercy, to take out all these roots from your life and replace them with his spirit of mercy, forgiveness, tolerance, and love.

In Jesus's name,

Amen

I Thought It Would Be Easier Than This

Papa, I can hear you calling
Papa, chains like rain are falling
Papa, blame is no longer mauling
Papa, rage is no more distorting
Papa, I can hear you calling.

But Abba, I thought it would be easier than this
You know, you being Father, me being your kid
Flowers and glories and outfits of grace
But it feels like an uphill struggle every single day
Technically, I guess that's how the Bible Jesus portrays
But he was divine and I'm just, well, human—made of "clay"
We can never compare, so why am I reaching for the impossible
up there?
I'm made in your image, but I'm not even a recognizable scar
I feel like a total distortion whilst you're total perfection, and
more
When I'm supposed to be free, I feel totally crushed
—smaller than the smallest grain of dust
Shorter than the words: "Not good enough"
Weaknesses and a body of sin to overcome, but knowing the
work will never be done
It won't ever be, till we're standing face-to-face
So, Father, whilst I'm earth how do I win this race? And not get
plagued by shame and guilt and disgrace?
How do I not fall or look away? How do I not give up on this
emotional game?
The mental arithmetic of being saved—the battles that are waged
in my mind, night and day
It's like having a thousand keys to only one lock—searching for
answers but always feeling lost
(I'm sure your gonna tell me all I have to do is knock!)
Trying to make life lessons out of why things have been this way,
then trying to balance them with your truth of mercy and grace

Where are the light and the way, instead of a different balancing
act every single day?
Or stretching and testing, as those pastors like to say—but,
Father, I feel like I wanna break
For ease, hoping all the effort and pain would slip away—but
knowing the latter end would be a thousand times worse than
today
Yes, for such thoughts, I should be ashamed—but you said never
to hide anything from your face
Plus, you know what I'm thinking in my heart anyways
So I'm presently my angst to you today
You're actually the only person that could take them away
I've constructed in my head how it should be
But from all my deliberations I'm still not in peace
So, it's a daily walk of holding onto grace? Wait, I thought grace
was holding me in place
Am I trying to play too many parts? Trying too hard to please?
You know being that Martha—whilst you say, "Sit at my feet"
Intentionally tracing in your Word the steps to take—but there
are no step-by-step instructions to navigate this my race
I know, that you're faithful in all that you say
I know, that your words will never pass away
So, I encourage my mind, but I'm starving my soul—I need more
than "soundbites" on which to hold
I need your healing—I actually want to be whole; I want to let
go—I want to rest and "be still and to know"
Not micromanaging past hurt and sin
Not etching out from your Bible where I'd best slot in
Ah, the ramblings of my heart, the wonderings of my soul—if
only they could decide and perfectly coincide
Maybe, surely then I'd have peace inside.

Ever felt like this?

_____

_____

_____

_____

_____

Exhausted from trying to work it all out: how to be in the world but not of the world, how to please God whilst loving everybody else, plus ourselves, of course! How to be an ambassador for Christ without judging others, how to delight in our achievements without coming across as proud. How to forgive other people and not expect anything in return. Trying to serve and desperately wanting appreciation and validation, and then trying to not feel guilty for feeling like this!

It can be so miserable trying to work out how we're supposed to live and what we're allowed to think and do. Most of us have been brought up in a very legalistic, rules-based version of Christianity and the church. And these legalisms, which promote rules over exercising wisdom and self-discipline, are the very things that Christ came to abolish. Calculating the parameters and boundaries of rules robs us of our time, our sanity, and our identity. Christ said we can live by grace, because he knows the nature and character of his spirit, which he put inside us when we accepted him. That spirit, the Holy Spirit, is more than a moral compass or guide. The Holy Spirit is the full power of God living inside us. He will prompt us and continually remind us of God's perfect will for our lives. It's his job to keep us on the path that Christ has laid before us.

So even if you do not trust yourself, at least trust what God has said he put inside you. God doesn't look at our actions or behaviors—he looks at our hearts. It's never about what we do, but why we do it. That is why rules cannot work. The same action could have two completely opposite motivations: one that's pleasing to God and one that is sinful. The Gospel of Luke, chapter 18, demonstrates this perfectly. Both men appeared to be doing the "right thing"; they were in the temple confessing their sins before God, but only one prayer was accepted. Why? Because one came from a heart of humility and the other from a heart of pride. Same actions, different results.

The only answer is to allow God's spirit to teach you his laws, precepts, and principles. Let yourself be schooled in the things that are truly pleasing to God.

MIND GAMES

My fears were like that raven from the ark, moving to and fro
with no place to go, looking to me for its home.
But your mercy said no, all doubt and fear had to go, your
righteousness had to grow, along with all the truth you'd sown.
And to let go, I also had to say no. I couldn't continue listening
to that radio of lies, of deceptions in disguise, transmitting
death in a comfortable tone, trying to make untruth my home.
Propaganda and Jesus slander, counterfeits trying to pull you
under, dead weights in angelic disguise, whispering torments and
dressing up lies.

Trying to ruin my identity in Christ, trying to defame your
character and name; trying to throw blame, trying to incite
shame, trying to maintain cause-and-effect, conjuring up images
of things that are dead, trying to instigate regret, trying to not let
me forget.
Tried but failed, *old things passed away*, new creature in Christ,
the daughter and bride, spiritually birthed, no longer from earth,
his blood in my veins—God's legitimate claim.

Reflect—Question—Ponder—Pray

You know, the devil is a real tormentor. He bombards you with images and thoughts of past mistakes, hurtful conversations, and things to make you feel sad and depressed. He does this on purpose—he's trying to make us feel condemned and ashamed, hoping we'll feel too "dirty" to go to God; hoping we'll give up, hoping we'll withdraw, stop going to church, and isolate ourselves. It's a tormenting spirit that makes people suicidal.

It can be demoralizing and draining trying to answer every accusation in your mind, and trying to justify and defend yourself. It can feel like agony and like your mind is under a constant barrage of attacks; like your thoughts and emotions are constantly being hijacked.

It can keep you awake at night and leave you irritable, suspicious, and difficult to be around. Many of us have lived this nightmare and during it thought we were the only ones, and that we were alone, but we're never the only ones. The devil has lots of different ways of targeting Christians, all to make us feel ineffective and alone.

But there is always a way out. We have a savior, Christ, with whom we must partner. We must take Christ's hand and step out of the pit. The reason we got there is irrelevant. The only important thing is getting out and staying out.

The first step is meditating on the Word of God. There is no other substitute. Find empowering scriptures to meditate and chew on, and repeat them in your head over and over for as long as it takes. Romans 8:15 and 1 Corinthians 2:16 are great scriptures to write down and start with.

_____

_____

_____

_____

_____

We have been given the mind of Christ and we must renew and strengthen it in his Word on a daily basis. Reading and meditating on the scriptures has the power to heal and deliver. It's not just a book, the Bible is living and active, and it was given to us to allow us to live victoriously.

My list of power scriptures:

_____

_____

_____

_____

_____

COMMITMENT FIRST

Commitment before privileges
Else you're sure to go broke
Broken expectations before getting a full quote
Exposing intricacies to those only in a queue
Not necessarily looking to you
Looking to whom will help them get through
Not looking at you—looking at what you can do
Ah, commitment before privileges
Or you're just the spoke to their wheel
What they give and take depends on how they feel
They'll always give to take then they'll show you their heel
It's to steal and kill, consuming your hard work—like a free meal
It's to steal and kill, riding on your back—to get the best deal
It's to steal and kill, they never truly cared how you'd feel
It's to steal and kill . . .

Commitment before privileges
Indulge in trust—don't make a paper plane of love
Don't send it careering into the ground—because you based your
affection on the wiles of a clown, because they didn't step over
you when you were down
Mimes and masqueraders, jesters at the ball
But when it comes to integrity they're barely two feet tall
Their opinion of you is *so* small
You gave them too much for nothing at all!

Reflect—Question—Ponder—Pray

This passage is really about discernment and trust. Balancing a
servant's heart with God's wisdom, to understand how much to
give, how much to receive, when to go the extra mile, and when
to pull back.

It's very easy to be naïve as a Christian and to easily get burned when people use you or take advantage. Even in these situations, it's reassuring to know we have a Father who will recompense us when we're unjustly treated.

Nonetheless, we can't act with blind love or blind faith. Tolerating is very different from condoning, excusing, or sweeping issues under the carpet.

Proverbs is an exhaustive book. It concentrates on God's principles of wisdom, revealing how "wisdom" acts and what "understanding" sounds like. It's a book we should all study, as wisdom is like wearing impenetrable armor; it protects us and allows us to advance forward.

Start by reading Proverbs 3. Write down all the things the Lord highlights to you. Think about how you can put some of these into practice.

_____

_____

_____

_____

Pick Up Your Mat And Walk

Victimhood is full of pride
You're just trying to feed the poor me inside
Enamored by your teary eyes
You're not looking for change—just casting more blame
Captivated by living in pain
Many different problems but the story's still the same
Asking for help, just to sing your songs of grief
Questioning God—not seeing the failings of your belief
Wake up to the deception—you're clothed in a web of lies
You're dancing with the devil and using sorrow as a disguise
Don't settle for pity when you can be resurrected and relieved
Stop making excuses and get on your knees
Don't you know we have a Father that answers every plea?
Don't you see we have a savior that took away those griefs?
Humble yourself in repentance and stand on his Word instead
Stop eating the bread of affliction and living as if you were dead.

Reflect—Question—Ponder—Pray

What were your first thoughts after reading this passage?

_____

_____

_____

_____

_____

Can you hear the tension? There is a lack of sympathy but also an air of jealousy; of, "What you're doing is not right," and also, "It's not fair that you can get away with acting like this."

_____

_____

_____

_____

Our Christian life is often like this. We can look at others and watch what they do with no apparent punishment or telling off from God, and then think, "Why am I even bothering?" But then we're quickly sobered by the Parable of the Talents. God doesn't judge us by comparing us to others. No, he looks at what he's given and asked us to do: *to whom much is given much is required!*

So what can we do when we feel like God's processing and working on us, whilst everyone else looks like they're on easy street? First, we have to stop looking at others. Despite outward appearances and behaviors, we will never know how someone else is living in their heart or mind; we can never judge the quality of someone's life from the outside. Secondly—yes, here comes our favorite word—we come before the Lord in repentance and ask him for the grace to walk our own unique journey. Thirdly, we can ask him for clarity and understanding, and we ask him what he's trying to teach us in this current season or phase of life. Finally, we can ask him to lift off any weights, false burdens or expectations we are carrying, which are not from him.

Whatever we pray, we do so in the name of Jesus, because the Gospel of John, chapter 14, tells us that anything we ask for in Jesus's name, the Father answers.

Amen

BUOYANT

Those wooden walls separated grace from hate, as the unseen was
made clean.
For all of me was shut away—for iniquity to be displaced and
authority take its place.
The grave clothes were washed away, but a bare skeleton still
remained—
Which had to be redressed; which had to be mended and
tenderly kept;
Which had to be clothed with heavenly bread and daily
deliverance fed.
Which had to receive words of life, which God's Holy Spirit
breathed from inside;
Which ignited understanding in my eyes and brought
enlightenment to my mind;
Which quickened a surrendering of will and rendered self-effort
permanently still;
Which moisturized me in grace and massaged me in the name
above names.

I sat up in that ark to realize I was awash at your feet—and your
tender love had gloriously and mercifully redeemed me. Now
awash in the beauty of your love, the crests of waves I see are
the surging torrents of your glory, the glistening gleams of your
majesty, the radiance of your throne, more glorious than any
treasure the earth has known.
Yet it's the tenderness of your caress that lets me know I am truly
blessed. It's the softness of your voice that blocks out every other
noise, it's the way you hold my head and how you put me safely to
bed that makes me understand—I'm always in yours, my Father's
hand.

Often, our experiences can feel like being shut away on an ark. Saying "yes" to God in the beginning seemed like such a good idea, but weeks, sometimes years later, you're still waiting for the "waters" to subside so that you can be released into your purpose and destiny.

God's waiting and incubation period is one of the most difficult parts of Christianity. There is a hidden tension in this passage, there's an acknowledgement that, yes, what God is doing is necessary and right, even though it hurts. Then follows a wave of adoration based on hope, and based on what is to come, and not what presently is. It's an adoration based on who God is, his character, and not on our understanding of him through our feelings. Hope tells our souls the truth about God, hope tells our minds to rest—it's impossible to figure God out. Hope is that bridge between where we are now and where God has promised we'll be. Hope causes us to worship God in advance, because we know he is faithful.

How do you reinvigorate hope when you're feeling weary from the journey?

_____

_____

_____

_____

_____

What do you think God is trying to develop in you during the wait?

Interment

When I was caught up in that ark, when all the earth seemed so
very dark
When the evil in me had to depart, when your rain beat heavy on
my heart
When your dove seemed like my only friend, and I wondered if
this phase would end
Whilst feeling hollow in that ark (your promises echoing off the
walls), whispering, "How long will this last?"
Determined not to tell myself there's still work to do, determined
to stay focused only on you.
Not blaming myself, your timing is true, and I know I have
been baptized anew. So I sigh, and walk, and return to the same
space, because I must let patience have her way—I was chosen to
operate in grace.
So I rest and rest again, and rest more, uncovering the layers of
what you have in store; understanding is not a tangible thing,
but a deep upwelling that surfaces within. It carries hearts and
thoughts, but it can't be explained, but others will know her by
your ways.
I knew what was wrong coming in, I knew outside of me were
corruptible things; but there's no secret or key to open these
doors; no mystery that must be found to clear away the clouds; no
revelation to stop the rain; no doctrines that must be ingrained;
no formula to be written down; no routine to recite out loud.
No logic with tangible signs; no feelings; no conceiving; no
predicting beginnings to determine an end; no answer to when.
On nothing it depends, on nothing related to me.
It will be, when you say.
You'll devise and determine that day.

Wrestling with God's sovereignty is a battle our minds can never win. It's about understanding that everything we do is by God's grace; our most shining moments are still the products of his grace being outworked in us. We also have to accept that our actions don't earn us "goodie points" with God. God responds to our obedience, he's not a puzzle we can figure out or a slot machine we can feed prayer and fasting into. God is sovereign; he decides what to do, how he wants to do it and when he wants to do it, all by himself. When we go looking for signs or try to force his hand, we can end up in a really dangerous place, exposing ourselves to deception and manipulation by the devil. (The devil is always lurking, waiting to tell you all the things you want to hear; that's why we have to learn to recognize God's voice and not just listen for the answers we want.)

The Bible tells us in the first chapter of Jerimiah that God watches over his Word to perform it. So if we are to mature, we need to move away from mentally trying to figure out how to make things happen and enter into Christ's rest, knowing that if God has said it, he will do it.

FALLIBLE

Astonishing, it's so easy to be deceived
So easy to think you're led by God
And sitting by his knees
So easy to believe what you've perceived
Making sense . . . but neglecting truth
Making plans on what you understand
Limiting God by not waiting on his truth
By not keeping his character to hand
If it's not his master plan
Then our works are born of man
It's so easy to be deceived
When we go by what we see.

Reflect—Question—Ponder—Pray

Do you have any experience of wrongly believing that you were being led by God?

It is so easy to feel inspired and assume it's God showing you the way. But this just means we've not been grounded in his Word. God never changes his mind or goes back on what he's said. He is God, he already knows every thought and decision that will ever be taken—nothing ever takes him by surprise.

We often get deceived when we ignore something God has said before, mainly because our desires outweigh our patience and trust in him. But when we read and study the Bible, we're taught the character of God. We can then use the scriptures to discern if something is biblical and of God, of our carnal, impatient flesh, or of the devil.

God always confirms his Word and everything he says is always in perfect alignment with the principles of the Bible. The Bible really is our protection and armor. Read the book of Ephesians and ask the Lord to teach you how to apply his Word in your day-to-day living.

Mountains

Declaring your truth within, not minding those outside things
Incubating the truth
Fellowshipping with you
Knowing it's a Father's love that can pull me through
Wanting so desperately to be loved by you
But knowing you do—accepting what your love is like
Not really sure if I've got it right
Deciding to honor that you live inside!
Of course, until the next time I burst out and cry.

Reflect—Question—Ponder—Pray

I'm reminded of the Parable of the Good Seed. Some fell on the path, others on rocky ground, some amongst thorns, and some into good soil. Our emotions reflect where God's Word has landed in our souls. It's so easy to receive words and revelations with joy, only for a contrary situation to come along and uproot it all.

God's Word becoming the truth in our lives takes practice—hearing and understanding it is just the first step. We then have to live and experience it, which means being tested to see if that Word has birthed any truth inside us. The good news is that once God's Word becomes part of our living, it can never be taken away from us. It's only when it's a seed that it's in danger; fruit is proof that the Word has been established.

How would you define your emotions (*e.g., erratic, temperamental, stable, numb, non-expressive*)?

_____

_____

How do you think those closest to you would describe them?

_____

_____

_____

_____

Do you feel confident and grounded when you've understood scripture, or does life cause you to doubt certain parts?

_____

_____

_____

Do you feel like you're living the fullness of life that Jesus died to give you? If not, why not?

_____

_____

_____

_____

This is a perfect opportunity to take what you've written above and release it into God's hands. Ask him to help you overcome any emotional or mental obstacle, and increase your faith so that his Word will bear fruit in every area of your life.

In Jesus's name,

Amen

How Can You Love One Like Me?

I didn't understand that the Bible was you speaking to me
You through your Word addressing all my hurts and needs
You by your spirit encouraging all you had made me to be
Determined to show Christ's identity is living in me
Uniquely created and wonderfully made—named and hairs
numbered by the ancient of days
Made in your likeness, formed by your hands—the wealth of your
creation, too marvelous to understand!
Declared your temple—the place you choose to dwell—making
your presence like a bottomless well
The majesty of your glory in this shabby jar of clay
What a loving Father—what a heart to treat us this way!

Reflect—Question—Ponder—Pray

Sometimes Christianity can seem so surreal and daunting. It's difficult to reconcile the world we live in and people's inherent mistrust with God's perfect love and Christ's sacrifice. On top of that, a heap of relationships with real people makes relating to our perfect God difficult. If we've not even experienced decent human love, how can we fathom a totally accepting, unconditional love?

It can often feel like you don't measure up, or you find it hard to believe that Christ finds you worthy of his love. And the truth is we're not worthy of it, but that didn't matter to God, he came for us anyway, because his love is not conditional—it's based on the depth and size of his heart. His is a love that covers a multitude of sins and keeps no record of wrongs.

Once again, a lot of words, but how do we make God's love real to us? How do we feel it?

There's only one way, we ask him: *God, show me your love, make it tangible and real for me, show me how to recognize your love, help me to enjoy it, help me to turn it from head knowledge into heart knowledge, help me to love you back.*

In Jesus's name,

Amen

Checklist For Change

Let my love be perfected in you, Lord
It's not a fight to live—it's a rest to be
It's difficult not living by what we see
But it's knowing my reality is you living in me
Perfect my love in you, Lord
I'm just trying to juggle all your stuff
Sometimes it's hard to see
That you don't want me to do, but just to be
Not to serve but to sit
Not to think but to live
Not to act just to stay
Yeah, it's actually always in your presence that I'm at ease
Hearing you speak makes me believe
I know you have nothing but love towards me
And I completely want to be free
It just feels like old habits are always bullying me
Help me to just be!

Reflect—Question—Ponder—Pray

We need to practice the art of sitting and being at ease in the Lord's presence. Nothing will transform us quicker than being in his company. A hundred prayer meetings cannot compare to honoring our God by making him the sole focus and dedication of our time and effort.

Make the commitment now to carve out an entire hour for God, starting with once a week. Don't feel the need to fill that time with activities, make time just to sit in his presence and wait for him to speak.

Day and time each week:

VICTORY SLIP

Trying to prove yourself is when you lose yourself
The fight's not in the flesh; it's not in trying to be the best
It's not in competing and passing tests
The victory is in Christ's rest
It's when it's his Word you thoroughly digest
In prayer it's the silencing of the will
In fasting it's the quietening of the soul
In believing—that's the fastening on of hope
When Christ's Word you can never let go
You've crossed over to finding whole
His words are the building blocks of our soul
His words made our body, his temple, and home.

Reflect—Question—Ponder—Pray

Reflect and make a list of all the things you've learnt about yourself
during this chapter:

_____

_____

_____

_____

_____

_____

If you knew the true power of the Bible and it's incredible ability to transform your entire life, down to the way you think, how you behave, the decisions you make, and how you feel about yourself, you would never put it down. The Bible is living and active; reading it can deliver you, studying it can heal you, and believing it will make you invincible to every attack and ambush of the devil.

Everybody wants to live a better Christian life, but you don't have to buy books and go to seminars to achieve this. Everything you need to understand God's Word; to use it, to pray it and to apply it to your life, is already inside you. God lives within us.

I implore you to consume and get to know the Word of God for yourself. Let it become heart knowledge and give yourself the chance to live, experience, and breathe the Gospel. Become the Gospel by letting the words of God reveal your true identity and purpose. There's freedom in that book, keep picking it up!

Having Your Will Crushed
And Yielding To God

"WHAT, THERE'S MORE?" I hear you say . . .

Because he is so just, God gives us a choice. He doesn't ask us to make a decision without the full knowledge of all the options. That is what the previous chapters were about, the washing and clearing out of everything that is not him. When our eyes have been opened; when we're free to see clearly because God has removed all the toxic fears and emotions from our lives; when we've been healed from our past and bad relationships, our lenses are no longer tainted or skewed. It's in this place of "soberness" that we can make the informed decision to really surrender our all to Christ.

God doesn't just want our obedience, he wants our cooperation—he wants us to trust him with our hearts, our lives, and our loved ones, friendships, and careers.

God becomes God in our lives when we put aside what we want for what he wants. We acknowledge that in his righteousness and power, he knows best. We accept that even our very best efforts are not good enough, and instead we choose to believe that all things will work together for our good, because we take him at his Word when he says he's our loving Father. We're mature enough to understand he corrects and disciplines us in love; that he's only ever saving us from ourselves, and the schemes of the enemy. We believe he is intentional in his love and that he doesn't pursue us only to turn around and make us jump through hoops. We accept that despite every other human, a relationship with him is unlike anything we've ever experienced. By his grace, we choose not to judge him or treat him based on how others have treated us.

Instead, we decide to let him take us by the hand and lead us into the life he designed and the desires he has for us. And we do this by walking by faith and not by sight.

God's ways are often contrary to human logic and societal norms. Increase is not always what the Lord calls an opportunity. So you're left with a choice to either be great at the things the world applauds, or to be great at that which heaven applauds.

Living Like You

You rose from the depths
And put captivity to shame
And through your suffering
You cemented your fame
Through the test, you were proved God's best
And endured it all to give us rest
You said we should do as you do
And follow in the perfect lifestyle ensampled by you
There's no reward for being patient when we've done wrong
Only when we're falsely accused, we must be strong
You didn't revile when you were blamed—you didn't taunt back
and call them names
You didn't utter a word—you had vowed to repeat only what you
heard the Father speak.

Reflect—Question—Ponder—Pray

This is our greatest call, to live by the same principles as Jesus. We've been given his spirit and mind, so we're equipped to walk in his examples of peace, tolerance, acceptance, and love.

Which aspects of Jesus's lifestyle do you find the most difficult to live up to?

_____

_____

_____

_____

_____

_____

Are you interested in pursuing Jesus further, or are you happy with where you are?

_____

_____

_____

_____

Take some time to reflect on those aspects of Christianity that seem impossible to you, then release them to the Lord in prayer.

It Can Be So Hard

Let the breeze of your Spirit blaze through
I am yearning to be caught up in you
I can see the entanglements that you've released from within
The webs of doubt, blockages of unbelief, the sin of how can it not
be done by me?
Father, I thank you for setting me free—for releasing me into who
you want me to be
What I thought would be grief is actually relief
Those feelings of dearth were from working the earth
I'm not lacking tools, I was lacking trust
Haunted by things passed away—haunted by what they would say
Trying to put pretty flowers on an imaginary grave
Trying to let them know it wasn't her fault, she tried and she
fought
Scared of walking in this new way—trying to figure it out, but
that only brings doubt
Forgetting I'm now brand new—forgetting I'm married to you,
but knowing your promises are true
So, Father, I'm calling out to you—I don't know how to walk in
this way, I don't know how to act and what to say
So, just carry me along your way
And just tell me every day, "We're doing OK."

Reflect—Question—Ponder—Pray

I'm not going to promise that submitting your will to God is going
to be easy. It's the step most Christians get stuck at, and it's why
so many are living way below God's best. Still, it all comes down
to the same paradox Adam and Eve faced in the garden: to trust
God or to go for something that looks better? Ultimately, that's
what surrendering looks like. It's letting go of all that we think is
good for us and trusting that what God has in store for us is more

than we could have ever imagined. When we pick up God's will, we commit to walking that road to its end, no matter what the journey looks or feels like. It takes nothing more than faith and trust.

If you feel your walk with God has become stagnated, it's worth considering if you're at this step—still trying to hold onto the bits of what you want to do and the bits of what God wants to do. But we can't have it both ways.

Are you ready to surrender your plans for God's will and purpose?

Mirror Mirror On The Wall

Prayer is not a wish list we throw in the air
It's not something we rush off then continue in worldly cares
Prayer is a weapon and an ornament of praise
Prayer declares, "My Father, I believe what you say!"
Prayer is a warfare against forces of evil and sin
Prayer tells the devil, "I'm in Christ, to you I'm never giving in!"
Prayer is a strategy we cannot pray amiss—
We have to get God's Principles right—prayer is not a tick list for
morning and night.
Prayer moves mountains and opens the skies—it's the foundation
for opening the eyes of the blind
It multiplies and raises what appears to be dead, and when
spoken in agreement ten thousand enemies are shed
"Forgive them, Father, they know not what they do,"—is the
prayer that saved both Gentiles and Jews!

Reflect—Question—Ponder—Pray

When we pray, it's to understand God's will—you're effectively asking for specifics.

Lord, what do you want me to do? What should I be focusing on this season? What are the things and relationships I need to let go of or lay down for a while? Lord, I'm feeling challenged in this area. How do I break through? Lord, what are you trying to teach me from this situation?

This is what a prayer sounds like, when it is prayed from the posture of surrender—you are purposefully seeking God's instructions and will.

How can you restructure your prayer requests to position yourself to hear God's will and plans for your life?

_____

_____

_____

COME TO ME

Come to me if you're seeking life
None will ever be denied.
Come to me and put off strife
Put off pain and hurt and lies.
Put off kicking against the wall
Put off striving to "have it all."
Put off lusts and selfish pride
Put off the troubles you have inside.
Put off repeating the same mistakes
Put off exhaustion in your day.
Put off foolish and offending words
Put off the cares that plague the earth!
Put off rejection and entanglement to sin
Put on my salvation, my glory brings you in.
Enter the promised land of truth
Where there is love and sound reproofs.
Where wisdom leads you by the hand
And understanding by you stands.
Where strength and might are internal things
And instruction lifts you up on wings.
Where the seeds you sow you'll reap
And the fruit you plant you'll eat.
Where my treasure won't decay
And favor brightens every day.
Where there's joy and ease in sleep
With justice singing in the streets.
Where the night is filled with peace
As every soul depends on me.
Here you'll always have a friend
I'm your rock, shield, and defense.

Surrendering your will means answering and saying yes to God's call over your life. Don't be mistaken. Being "called" is not just the reserve of church leaders. We are all called by God for a specific purpose in his kingdom. You may be called to run an ethical and sustainable business in a notoriously corrupt industry; you may be called as an EA (Executive Assistant) for a Fortune 500 CEO to demonstrate integrity. We are all called to at least one of the seven cultural mountains of society: media; arts and entertainment; religion; government and politics; family; education, and business. Every single child of God has an assignment on one of these mountains. You have a kingdom purpose and mandate, which God has specifically and uniquely designed you for.

If you're suffering from any of the symptoms mentioned in the first half of this passage, it's an indication that you're still trying to live and operate according to your own desires and in your own strength. As soon as you fully step into alignment with God, the grace and all the provisions, connections, intelligence, skills, and finances required in order to fulfill your destiny will be supplied.

Did you know about the seven cultural mountains of society?

_____

_____

_____

_____

_____

_____

Do you know which of these you are called to operate in?

_____

_____

_____

_____

_____

If not, ask the Lord to reveal this to you through a personal revelation, and to give you added assurance by confirming it through someone else (the Lord always confirms his Word). You can pray:

> Lord,
>
> Thank you for letting me know I have a kingdom purpose and destiny. I'm sorry for all the ways I've been acting in my own strength, according to my own will. Father, in your mercy and love, realign my heart, will, mind, motives, ambitions, and desires with yours. I want to dedicate my life to finding out and living out your perfect will for me. Father, give me the grace to walk in your will and open the eyes of my understanding so I may know with confidence which of the seven mountains you've called me to. Father, open every door and opportunity so that I may advance according to your plans and close every door that isn't your perfect will for me.
>
> In Jesus's name,
> Amen

MY SHIELD AND BUCKLER

When silence was my daily bread and meditation my bed
And in your Word I lay my head—
remembering all you've said
Resting in your courtyard of grace
Allowing your presence to infuse and bathe
Reciting the precepts of ancient of days
Filling the air with declaration and praise
Singing the darkness away
Covering myself with your many names
Drawing out shield and bow
By letting you let me know
You're always in control.

Reflect—Question—Ponder—Pray

God is in control. This is something we have to speak into our emotions and soul when they are screaming at us to take the easier route via a wider path.

God has never fallen off his throne. He has never failed. He has and always will know what he is doing. We see things from a simple myopic view, whilst God sees everything that is connected to us in the present and future, and he is masterfully orchestrating everything so it will come together for our good, and the good of those around us.

You may be thinking, "God, I really want this job, as it will make the finances at home easier." Whilst God could be thinking, "I really want an influencer whose decisions will bring ease to organizations and communities." God's mind, scales, and ambitions for us are way above our wildest imaginings. Plus, despite what we may think, only he knows what will give us deep, long-lasting joy and satisfaction. The majority of the things we reach for have fleeting or short-lived pleasures, and then we're back to where we started, looking for the next pick-me-up or adventure. When we step into God's plans we will not lack any good thing, because we're partnering with the creator of our likes and souls!

Notes:

_____

_____

_____

_____

_____

As Weak As I Am

What can my hands do anyway—they were made from dust?
Everything they touch without your blessing will surely rust
Everything they try to make without your trust will ensnare
Would drown out righteousness with their worldly cares and
tares.

So I let go—to let your perfect will flow
I take a seat—and you rise up on the inside of me
I go to sleep—as you've subdued everything under your feet
I rise to eat—as you've prepared the way and planned my day
I read your Word—because it's the most precious thing in this
world
I let you speak—because it's communion with you that makes me
meek
I let myself be weak—because you promised that through that I
would be complete.

Reflect—Question—Ponder—Pray

How successful have your attempts been at establishing a good life
for yourself?

_____

_____

_____

_____

_____

Has the success been in every area of your life? (*For example, has it impacted your mind, emotions, heart, spirit, career, family, finances, relationships, health?*) Have you managed to impact all these or just experienced partial success in some areas?

_____

_____

_____

_____

_____

When we endeavor in our own strength, we get what we put in on a 1:1 ratio. But when we partner with God and work according to his purpose, we step into multiplication, where one seed can reap a hundred-fold harvest. Everything of God produces lasting fruitfulness; nothing decays, falls apart, or causes disappointment, regret, or pain. God's riches never come at the expense of somebody else or the environment, equity, or justice.

The areas where we feel most successful are typically the hardest to surrender to God, as it doesn't "look like" we need help. It's easy to ask for help in areas where we know we are weak, or where things are failing.

But today I want us to be bold and offer up these most treasured areas, acknowledging even our best and most celebrated achievements are limited when compared to God's ability and greatness.

> Father God,
>   I choose today to lay down and surrender those aspects of my life I hold most dear; my greatest accolades,

achievements, joys, and proudest moments. I release all
control over to you, knowing that in your hands the little
I have to offer will abound to your glory and be a blessing
to more people than I could ever reach. Help me, Lord, to
trust and lean on you, and give me the grace to allow you
to be God over every area of my life.

In Jesus's name,
Amen

Perceiving Truth

You wash away our old and give us your new
It's a righteous gift—still it comes with reproof
To keep us safely aligned in the ways of you
To keep us from being deceived, from losing truth
That's the most the enemy can do—defame the character of you
To alter our path from the certainty of your sovereignty and bible proof
He makes evil by the decisions he brings—trying to force us to make mistakes
But you've enlightened our every step and cleared our every way
And given your Word as a shelter, shield, and shade
Your love he can never break—letting you die on the cross was his greatest mistake
And now it's the authority of your name we take
So we end with nothing less than your best
So we finish our race to your perfect rest.

Reflect—Question—Ponder—Pray

A difficult part of our Christian walk is accepting we have an enemy in the devil, who the Bible says is out to steal, kill, and destroy. He is actively working against us to throw us off track and poison our relationship with God.

This isn't an easy thing to accept. We'd all much prefer to just cover ourselves with the blood of Jesus and believe we're totally immune to the forces of darkness. But it doesn't work like that, because God has called us heirs of salvation and has put his very own spirit within us. This means he has enabled us to overcome all that is in operation in the world, in the same way Jesus overcame death.

Write out what 2 Corinthians 2:11 tells us:

_____

_____

_____

_____

If we are going to accept God's call on our lives, we have to understand that the forces of darkness want to oppose us. They don't want our God-given light in their dark places. The light of Christ that we carry exposes evil and corruption; it has the power to tear down walls of intolerance and hate, as well as bring hope and solutions.

So how do we overcome and persevere? Well, we feed ourselves on the Word, it is our armor (Ephesians 6) and instruction manual (books of Philippians, Colossians, James). The greatest weapons you have against the devil and his cohorts is the Word of God, believing what God has said and standing on that truth, no matter what you see around you in the natural world. This is how we obtain victory.

The devil engineers situations and circumstances to steal our belief (faith) and the truth of who we are in Christ (our identity). When we remain steadfast and refuse to be bullied out of our destiny, we will successfully advance and our peace and joy will never be shaken again, because they're rooted in Christ through his Word.

Reflections:

_____

_____

_____

_____

TENDERLY TRANSFORMED

You open our eyes of unbelief
And in their place you shower your peace
Rest, rest, rest is our daily grain
We have to believe in your able name
Resting, believing in you—it's acting in your truth
It knows you'll always come through
It knows you're righteous in everything you do.

Resting means no defense of self
No figuring it out or competing with everyone else
It's knowing you're above all else!
So in your presence simply we dwell
Knowing instructions come when we are meek
Knowing in you we always find what we seek.

Reflect—Question—Ponder—Pray

The book of James talks about how vicious and violent our tongues are. They make great boasts and, like a struck match, can wreak immeasurable damage.

Our tongues, even when they're not being directly confrontational, can still delay and subvert our destinies. We know that the Bible tells us that the power of life and death is in our tongue—there is creative and destructive power in the words we speak. Our words can come into alignment with God and work for us, or they can work against us and uproot all our good efforts and advancements. If we desire to mature and walk in the fullness of God's will, then being masters over what we say is imperative.

When are you most prone to speak rashly or negatively?

_____

_____

_____

_____

On a scale of 1-10, how positive and life-giving are the words you speak? Why that score?

_____

_____

_____

_____

_____

The Bible tells us that out of the heart the mouth speaks. How are you filling your heart with God's Word?

_____

_____

_____

WILLFUL

Hope prepares us to hear your Word
Knowing our pleas are always heard
You're not a Father who turns away
We're always extended in your perfect grace
Waiting stretches and sharpens our resolve
Knowing the end has already been told
Faith enriches our spirit man
In every battle we're stronger to stand
Trust defends against all storms
You never forsake us and never let us fall
You're faithful in every word of your call
Your burden is light—you came to give rest to all.

Reflect—Question—Ponder—Pray

I'll say it again, there's no substitute for reading and studying the Word. Anything of quality or worth in life requires sacrifice, focus, training, practice, commitment, investment, and study. It's the same for God's Word. Studying the Bible isn't as daunting as it seems. Here are three simple steps to get you started on a journey of discovery, amazement, and reverence:

1. Pray for understanding, illumination, and light.

2. Read and allow the Holy Spirit to highlight scriptures to you, note them down.

3. Take the highlighted scripture and use what you understand from it in a prayer.

Process Progress

Truth has been accomplished
That means success has been achieved
All that was required was for me to just believe.
Hope has been embodied
And destiny can now be seen
There's beauty for our ashes
Burnt has been turned to evergreen!

Reflect—Question—Ponder—Pray

Having our will crushed by God marks the transition between only seeking his hand to seeking his face, glory, and presence.

I'll give you an example. When people desire to marry, it's common for them to make a wish list of their top wants; some even go as far as thinking about how they were treated in past relationships and then note down the qualities that would make up for these past experiences. People can be very specific and know what type of look, career, income bracket, and even what hobbies they would like their potential spouse to possess, as well as how that person would make them feel. The funny thing is, you never hear what they want to be able to do for their future special someone—you never hear how they intend to serve them!

Don't get me wrong, desiring marriage is healthy, but what can be unhealthy are the self-orientated and self-serving motivations behind any of our desires.

I want you to take the time to be really honest with yourself. Search your heart and write down any selfish ambitions or desires that you're still holding onto.

_____

_____

_____

_____

_____

_____

Often, God wants to give us the things we desire, but it's more of his heart to bring us to a place where our motivations are in line with his, so that we don't end up misusing or abusing the very thing we've been asking him for.

DON'T GROW WEARY IN DOING GOOD

To bring forth righteousness, rain does wet the soil
And from our dead seeds, life begins to uncoil
Birth pushes through the growth, as it heard the heavens speak
So it races to the sound of light and rushes from its roots beneath
Bursting through the dirt and the soggy ground
It explodes into the earth—new life it has found!
Crowned with sunshine and clothed with wind
The rays of light cause growth within
Forever reaching to greet its king
What marvelous fruit this tree does bring
A shelter, a home, a cooling shade—
All because this seed obeyed.

Reflect—Question—Ponder—Pray

This is the crux of living out our full Christian identities; we must first die to self before Christ can resurrect something new. The Gospel of John, chapter 12, tells us plainly that if a grain of wheat falls into the ground, it will forever remain alone, but if it dies it will bring forth much fruit.

Upon salvation, we became that grain of wheat, and to become fruitful we have to go through the organic process of death, incubation, re-birth, growth, development, maturity, then fruitfulness. Dying to self is a continual process of saying "yes" to God and "no" to yourself—there are no shortcuts.

If it's not a journey you're willing to take, if you're too attached to your comfort zone and prefer the quick-wins and those instantaneous feel-good factors, then God still loves you just as much. However, always know that he desires so, so much more for you, and his invitation to come up higher is always open.

Stay blessed

Remembering The Heart Of Our Father

With everything we've talked about and covered so far, this chapter is really about re-anchoring ourselves in what God is to us. It's not just about who God is, but what he means to us in real terms, in our day-to-day lives.

These are the reminders and testimonies, and the truths and comforts we hold onto when life circumstances are trying to eat away at our faith and strength.

When situations are trying to push you down or talk you out of your purpose and destiny in Christ, the following pages will give you the confidence and foundation to stand tall.

It's my hope that you'll connect with the Lord on a deeper, more fulfilling level. I'd love you to come to understand his heart and thoughts towards you, leaving you feeling totally secure and accepted. It's God's genuine desire to see you prosper and excel in life.

You're blessed!

A Love That Doesn't Look
At Wrong Or Right

I celebrate you, Father, as king
I bask in the joy of the glory you bring
For you numbered all of our sins, you tallied them up from the
days we'd live in
You measured how we would transgress
You counted, us being the less of our best
You drew out all our distress
And what it would take to be out of our mess
What it would take to be rid of sin stress.

It took greater than the sum of all parts
It needed one with an above-human heart
One that was never intimidated or moved by the dark
Who wasn't afraid of human-made scars
Who would touch the unclean, secured in his being
Restored by your giving, to love was your living.

To love was your living
It's the transformation I step in
It's your love that I'm changed in
It's where I no longer love sin
In fact, I'm selflessly found within
A love that makes the angels sing
A love that no human could ever bring
It's a love where I found life
And the power to be the greatness you put inside
It's a love that doesn't look at wrong or right
But just tries to ignite your grace and your light
It's a love that kisses me to sleep every night
Knowing you win me every battle and fight
It's a love that doesn't look at wrong or right
It looks to the Father, who opened our eyes
Who freed us from captives and put his spirit inside

Your love is what's right
Only your love has the power to transform lives
Yours was the only love that chose to die
A love that laid down its life
A love renamed as Christ.

Reflect—Question—Ponder—Pray

What were your thoughts whilst reading this passage?

_____

_____

_____

_____

What are the things that remind you that Christ loves you?

_____

_____

_____

_____

Touch Of Love

If every human paid, the sin was too great; it wasn't enough
It needed the most precious and pure
It needed significant God-quality blood
It needed the heavy weight of divine
A magnificent king, with healing in his wings.

Who would touch a mess or decay
You knew a touch would cast sin away
You knew a touch was deeper than saying our name
A touch said, "You matter to me"
It frees us from all manner of insecurities.

A touch makes us whole
And makes us know we're totally known.

You said that in love was a fight
A battle of what's good in your sight
What actions and words breed light
How forgiveness ignores wrong or right
It's in staying connected there's life.

Reflect—Question—Ponder—Pray

Can you think of a time when God used someone else to really
bless you and let you know how much you're loved?

The Thought Of You

Your love is a mighty spear
That pierces every concern and worry of the soul
Your care is a sharp arrow
It hits its mark, always knowing where to go
Your attention is like oil
It seeps underneath every closed door
It permeates every rusty place
The residue and fragrance of you cannot be faked
It gets into our most delicate and intricate place
Your affection is like soap
It lathers and washes away—it indulges and bathes
Your kindness is softer than wool
Your gentleness lighter than dew
Your salvation like warmth from the sun on our brow
Your name a shelter wherein we can forever lie down.

Reflect—Question—Ponder—Pray

Can you think of a time when God rescued you from a sticky or terrible situation?

_____

_____

_____

_____

OUR FATHER

Your heart, my Father
Yearns for those who are lost
Each beat weeps for those poor sheep, who've wandered far from
home
Who are cold and all alone, who stumble upon the stones.

Your love, my Father
Searches each valley and hill
It doesn't stop and it will never yield—it's looking for those to
heal
Looking to save those the wolves would kill.

Your arm, my Father
Plucks them from the pit
When they fight and they resist—alas, your Mercy still persists
What manna of love is this?

Your call, my Father
Mends every broken bone
Carries every lost sheep home—bathes the neglected whole
Then sets them beside your throne.

Your heart, my Father
Yearns for those who are lost
So found them through a cross
Paying the total cost.

Reflect—Question—Ponder—Pray

Can you think of a time when God showed you incredible mercy,
so that you didn't have to face the consequences of a mess you'd
gotten yourself into?

UNDEFEATED CHAMPION OF THE WORLD

A tournament ensued for my life—and you took my place in the
fight.
You entered that ring willing to die—you counted me the final
prize.
You took the blows, bruises, and cuts—your only fear was not
showing your love.
You wanted the entire world to see—that it was worth it all, dying
for me.
You took the jeering from the crowd—and how they mocked
when you fell down.
They thought it over in the count—your bones and blood were
pouring out.
You spilt your life upon the ground—and they just sneered and
all walked out.
Saying that there was no doubt—your name of light had flickered
out.

But then your glory tore the ground—an empty grave is all they
found.
Your opponent, now chained in defeat—paraded shamefully
through the streets.
Your victory, it was not delayed—you prophesied it would be
three days!
Crowned in righteous robes of red—declared the first fruits of the
dead.
Risen and ascended king—seated, rested from everything.
Gloried in your finished works—magnified for saving earth.
Prince of peace, eternal life—Christ the blessed crucified.

What a savior; always there for us, forever interceding and fighting on our behalf. What a wonderful God to serve!

How does this passage make you feel about your future, knowing that Christ is indisputably on your side?

_____

_____

_____

_____

_____

Aha!

The strategies of the enemy have come to naught
The blood of Jesus Christ redeemed and bought
"Not guilty," is proclaimed in every court
"I'm free!" exclaimed by all who sought . . .
Who sought your face, your arm, your ways
Who sought to find your narrow gate
Who left off sin and worldly games
Who suffered solely for your name
Who looked within your Word for hope
Looking to you to break their yokes
Knowing it was freedom that you professed
Knowing a Christ confession put off death
Waiting to live your very best
With your breastplate of righteousness upon their chest
Knowing you were God and were true
Waiting to be delivered and rescued by you . . .
Salvation saves us from death
Deliverance raises our head
It puts every claim of the enemy to bed
It's redeeming your inheritance by the blood that was shed
It's the becoming of being brand new
It's partnering with Christ in spirit and truth.

Reflect—Question—Ponder—Pray

Assured that in Christ we can conquer all, what impossible dreams can you now believe in?

DUTY AND LOVE

It pained you to see us enslaved,
for you had given us dominion in those first seven days.
So Christ had to come and redeem,
so your mercy in spirit and truth could be seen.
The power of Christ none perceived,
as such love, no heart or mind could conceive.
The inheritance of the now seated king,
through your blood and belief we now enter in.

Reflect—Question—Ponder—Pray

Read Psalm 89

What did you understand from it?

THE GREAT INSTEAD

Jesus, you justified me, you made me, and you set me free
You kept me, you loved me, and you sanctified me
You bathed me, you clothed me, and fed me my daily bread
And you did it all for nothing, I said
In fact, you are The Great Instead
You died Instead
You cried Instead
Was scorned Instead
Forlorn Instead
Denied Instead
Flesh torn Instead
With thorns Instead
You mourned Instead
Still you called Instead—I'll pay their debts, I'll take the blame
Father, put on me their shame! Yes, write their balance to my
name
This wager they could never bear—So, Father, I will take their
share!
Chastised Instead
Despised Instead
Abused Instead
And bruised Instead
Maligned Instead
You cried Instead—Forgive them, Father, for what they do
I just want them reconciled to you—to darkness, they should
never lose
So I'll bear this cross so they can choose.

Reflect—Question—Ponder—Pray

In a world full of so many "pretenders," isn't it great to have a
proven savior!

Of all the sacrifices listed above, which spoke to you the most? Which one are you most grateful for?

_____

_____

_____

_____

_____

BE OF GOOD CHEER

As beautiful as a rainbow displayed by the splendor of your light
Is the peace of your instruction in the depths and still of night
As calming as the water's flow, by the valleys in the brooks
Is the knowing that no detail of our life has been overlooked
As gentle as a petal feels against the skin
Is the overwhelming assurance, we're no longer bound to sin
The immutable fact that your words none can retract
Sends every fear and doubt and devil running back
Your covenant of grace—because Jesus took our place
Summits every challenge that in life we're bound to face
When we are weak, in us you stand tall
And you speak to our souls, "I overcame it all."

———————————————————————

Reflect—Question—Ponder—Pray

Reflections:

————————————————————————

————————————————————————

————————————————————————

————————————————————————

————————————————————————

————————————————————————

Jubilation!

Arise!
And see the glory of the king
You'll see him in the promises he brings
You'll catch him with your unnatural eye—you'll miss him if you look for signs
Leap up!
He'll catch you on his wings—his covering, with him healing brings
He'll quicken spirit, mind, and soul—he broke his body to make yours whole
Stretch Out!
Your stakes, enlarge your tent—the battle's over, Christ's blood was spent
It overcame, redeemed, restored, and Christ's inheritance waits in store
Bow down!
And recognize your king
The sovereign Lord, will you let him in? Your master's standing at the door
You said yes once . . . will you bow for more?

———————————————

Reflect—Question—Ponder—Pray

How well do you think you trust God?

———————————————

———————————————

———————————————

_____

_____

What experiences have built up and added to this trust?

_____

_____

_____

_____

_____

Do you believe he has more in store for your life?

_____

_____

_____

_____

Only You Alone

Wash us from the poison we eat
And cleanse us from where we tread our feet
Bring to remembrance you created us unique
So let you be the riches we seek.

Rid us of our clothes of decay
Which expose our vulnerabilities, tears, and shame
Let our garments be truth and light
Clothed with the discernment of what's wrong and what's right.

Cover our ears from lies and deceit
Let false words never be found when we speak
Cause us in wisdom to choose the company we keep
And to walk by faith and act in belief.

Reflect—Question—Ponder—Pray

What stands out for you most in this passage?

_____

_____

_____

_____

_____

_____

Christ Says Follow Me There

OUR JOURNEYS, OUR CHRISTIAN lives, are about sacrifice. They are about following Christ into cold and dark places, because this is where his love and light are needed the most. Jesus famously said that those who are well have no need of a physician.

The people that the Lord is asking you to serve and be a blessing to are going to be sick. Whether that's spiritually sick because they don't know Christ, emotionally sick (making them spiteful or hateful), or mentally sick. Either way, we're called to love everyone—we are all made in the image of God!

Picking up our cross and following Christ means laying down everything else: promoting, avenging, and defending ourselves. It means being obedient to Christ above all and being silent when he says be silent, even when falsely accused. To work unto him and not unto man (even if you are being taken advantage of), and to always forgive and turn the other cheek.

We don't do these things because we are superhuman or emotionally immune—not at all. We do them in obedience because we trust God. We trust that he will always avenge us, re-compensate us, and restore all that was taken from us. And we trust him to do these things in his own time and in his own way. We put our hope in him, and not in our own efforts to sort things out.

Picking up your cross is an incredible journey—you'll find things out about yourself you never knew. You'll rise up in triumph over the things that used to crush you. You'll dust off the temptations that used to have you bound in cycles of condemnation and sin. You'll see God show up for you in every aspect of your life—simply because you gave him the room to do so.

Above all, you'll see that his mercy, favour, and grace have already gone ahead and prepared a way for you.

Your greatest testimonies and triumphs are still to come.

Let's march forward to that upward call of Christ.

AFFLICTED ADORATION

Everyone wants the solution; no one wants to pay the price
Erm . . . haven't you read the Bible? Didn't you see the life of
Christ?
Regarded not his divinity, clothed in the skin of man, humbled
himself through obedience—the sinless, spotless lamb
Suffered all indignities, slaughtered on a cross—innocent of all
the accusations, still he chose to pay our cost
Everyone wants the solution; no one wants to pay the price
Looking for a shortcut, I didn't see any in the life of Christ
Daily in the temple, steeped in a life of prayer, listening to the
Father— operating through love and care
Only rebuking evil, tempted but never yielding to sin—all for the
precious promise of presenting us before the king
Everyone wants the solution; no one wants to pay the price
Not knowing we're the debtors to the precious blood of Christ.

Reflect—Question—Ponder—Pray

It's easy for people to look at aspects of our lives and be envious,
with no understanding of what they cost us. If you could write to
your younger self about embarking on this journey with Christ,
what advice would you give yourself?

_____

_____

_____

_____

MAJESTY

Your authority was never displaced
Your sovereignty never dethroned
You were the one that let your life go
The heavens would have tore open—if you had said so
In the gentleness of your majesty we see—we're called to live life,
sacrificially
It's not about what others perceive—it's about being who you
created us to be
Heaven is cheering whilst the crowds on earth are jeering
The Father's applauding whilst the mockers here aren't lauding
We shouldn't be falling to be approved on earth—we shouldn't be
moved by what they deem worth!
Our lives would never be the same, if we choose, like Jesus, to
only obey what we hear the Father say.

Reflect—Question—Ponder—Pray

It's not about what others perceive—it's about being who God created us to be. How do you feel about this statement? Did any of it challenge you?

Following Christ's principles can mean being mocked, slandered, laughed at, and excluded. What's your strategy for overcoming situations like these?

_____

_____

_____

_____

_____

In The Still

Here, your laws have been written on my heart
Not in the battle but in the still
Not when faced with death, but when I kneel
When my breathing is slow and
When I'm all alone
It's then you make yourself be known.

To the rhythm of my beating heart
You're scribing promises of light
To the silence of my mind
You've bound up truth, where there once bore lies
You've cleared my ears, which were clogged with fears
You spoke and all my doubt eloped
You erected your temple and made my body your home
In the still
Between the pages of your end from your beginning
You ploughed a space for me
In Christ's grave you planted a seed
Because it was always your heart to raise me
In the still
Through the cold, dark earth you were whispering nutrients of
love
Calling me up, calling me above
In the still
Through the dampness of regret
Through if, when, why, and not yet
In the still
When the soil had crushed my will
When to live it meant to yield
In the still.

Reflect—Question—Ponder—Pray

What does being still before God look like to you?

_____

_____

_____

_____

_____

Being still also means taking every decision, issue, endeavor, and idea to God first, soliciting his opinion above everyone else's. Being still means we wait for his answer and instructions before moving on.

Which of these two do you struggle with the most? Why do you think that is?

_____

_____

_____

_____

_____

THE MASTER'S PLAN

Deeper, deeper is your call
Always wanting us to know more of you
Always calling us to see what you can do
So we can be confident and assured in you
You said, "Don't contend," you said, "Just pray"
Praying your prayers is what paves the way
It's what empties the grave
It's always about saying what you say
I don't have to fight with my words
When I can pray with my heart
I don't have to strive and curse
It's in the spirit we move this earth
Committing everything to you
And watching you do what only you know how to do
Watching everything you created fall down to you.

Reflect—Question—Ponder—Pray

Deep calls to deep, the Bible says; the Father is always calling us into more; into a more intimate relationship, into less and less of ourselves, so that we can be filled up with more of him.

In which areas do you believe the Lord is asking more of you?

_____

_____

_____

_____

_____

_____

What actions can you take to enrich and deepen your prayer life or prayer frequency?

_____

_____

_____

_____

_____

THE ACT OF WAIT

We pray, we watch, we wait
We don't try and make things happen with cunning words nor
debate
We don't contend with fists of words—we just wait patiently on
what we've heard
Not using our mouths to disturb the precious seeds of your Word
We pray, we watch, we wait
Knowing your Word you never forsake
You perform every word you say
You don't make mistakes—every one of our days you've already
written down on page
We're just waiting for you to blow them our way
Receiving your will—they're buried in prayer
Knowing good fruit is guaranteed there
Knowing you water us with your heavenly care
We pray, we watch, we wait.

Reflect—Question—Ponder—Pray

Patience is the discipline that brings forth precious and long-last-ing fruit. Everything God wants to do with us will require us put-ting our emotions, impulses, and desires in subjection to patience.

Patience builds character and trust; it also exposes what's at the core of our belief. Some people have had to wait thirty years for a promise from God to materialize. We live within the confines of time, but God doesn't. The Bible tells us that a day is as a thou-sand years and a thousand years is as a day to God. We measure ourselves according to time, whilst God looks at the maturity and state of our hearts.

We saw the consequences of impatience in the lives of Sarah and Abraham; and their attempt to help God give them a son, which resulted in Ishmael. Ishmael came into being because of the work and efforts of a limited and impatient human mind and will. Isaac was the promise! It's hard to imagine the pain this situation caused, which eventually ended in Ishmael and his mother (the bond woman) being sent away. We often get into messy and difficult situations when we try to rush ahead of God.

What would you do if you found out that what you wanted from God would take another thirty years to materialize? How would you feel?

_____

_____

_____

_____

_____

The Weight Of Wait

You wash away the old and give us your new
There's no questioning of from whom—we've found everything in
you
There's no striving with man—trying to get the upper hand
In your spirit we understand—you've devised the master plan
We just have to follow through in obeying you
Whilst we let you do what only you can do.

Wisdom sits until instructions come
Faith acts on what can't be undone
Fear stalls and arrogance runs
So we must be spirit led
To actualize your plans
We must be spirit led
To hear and understand
We must be spirit led
To be maneuvered by your hand.

Reflect—Question—Ponder—Pray

Are you in a church where they welcome and wait on the Holy
Spirit?

_____

_____

_____

_____

Are you more comfortable with the knowledge that God is still speaking to us as his sons and daughters?

_____

_____

_____

_____

Do you want to hear more of God for yourself? This often requires shutting down other sources of noise and interference, i.e., giving up some TV, social media, and magazines. Is this a sacrifice you're willing to make?

_____

_____

_____

_____

_____

RECEPTIVE TO REST

What does rest look like? It involves not making rules
It involves a freedom in all you've called us to do
A willing surrender—it's not a giving up
It's placing our all and everything in your trust
If you woke us up in the morning, there's a purpose to the day
It's the continued abiding in that you would have your way
What does rest look like? It's a call to grace
It's a surpassing joy that no effort can replace
What does rest look like? It's our head in your lap; it's our sitting
at your feet
It's a knowing that listening to you, Master, is what makes
everything complete.

Reflect—Question—Ponder—Pray

Rest in this context is not the opposite of activity. Rest is a mind-frame and heart position. It's about being rooted in the victory Christ has already won. Rest means taking God at his Word—it's not about trying to work it out for yourself or trying to help him out. It's not about being inactive, it's more of an unwavering conviction that God will do exactly as he has promised, and it's your job to be moved—not by your feelings or other people's opinions, but by his instruction alone.

You can be very busy and still be at rest because your confidence is not in what you're doing or achieving, but rather in Christ and his words and promises.

Can you recognize the areas of your life where you are/are not operating from rest?

_____

_____

_____

_____

_____

Ask the Lord to teach you how to sit at his feet and enter his rest.
  In Jesus's name,
  Amen

ASCENDING

I rose from the depths of self
Effortlessly ascending on your love
Weightless—you've taken all my cares
Buoyant—you cut away those Tares
I'm no longer a puppet to the flesh of death
No longer underfed and underpaid
No more exchanging of life for a deadly wage
Just floating on your truth, arising further by your teaching and
reproofs
Gliding higher by just focusing on you
Soaring to your upward call
Knowing I could never fall
Taking hold of you
Further bolstered by your Word
Sustained by your spirit of might
Knowing your very breath swallowed death
Assured this will all end with your very best
Flying by your victory
Elevated to your rest.

Reflect—Question—Ponder—Pray

What did this passage say to you?

Purposed Prayer

When we can touch, see, and smell it—then we turn our prayers
to praise
It's after we receive the promise that we should start to celebrate
Praying is not the victory—it's praying until we see it come
through
It's being diligent in your reverence and service to God, and
giving him no excuse
We pray his promises back to God—we pray for revelation in our
heart
We pray to understand his ways—and mature us to finish what
we start
We pray to uproot our habits of sin—we pray before any endeavor
we want to begin
We pray because we're human and we will always get it wrong—
We pray because where we are weak, he's eternally strong
We have to pray according to your will, Father—you always
answer prayer
Stop us from going round in those circles of: "Is there anybody
there?"
Prayer is about discovering what you, Father, want for our lives
Forgive us for our blindness, Lord, and . . .
in your mercy, open our eyes!

Reflect—Question—Ponder—Pray

Comparing where you are now with how you were before. Have
your views on prayer changed? What is your current understanding of the purpose of prayer?

Prayer 101

When we pray according to your promises, there's always a
release
The part we don't understand is—that's when comes the "beast"
To intercept and destroy what heaven's already deployed
We must intercede and stand until we see angelic hands—
Evil overthrow and bring your yes or no
Pray without ceasing was not said in vain—we pray for the
answer then we pray it comes our way
The devil, you told us, seeks to steal and destroy—
So we pray through his attempts to sabotage and dispel
You always answer prayers, Lord, let us never be deceived
And you always want to give us the things we truly need
Help us continue in prayers, Lord, until your answers seen
Help us hear your "No's" Lord, when we feel we ain't received!

Reflect—Question—Ponder—Pray

Does such a thing as unanswered prayer exist? Or do we miss
God's response because we're only listening and looking out for
the answers we want?

God answers our every prayer; sometimes it's a yes, sometimes it has conditions, often it's a no—and those no's have reasons. Sometimes he tells us to wait or we get a gentle "not yet." Many times he'll tell us that the thing we're asking for is not really the thing we need, or that what we are asking for will end up hurting us or draw us away from him in the long run.

God always answers every request, so ask him to open your ears and heart to all his responses!

Peace Has Friends

Fruit and blessings fall to earth
Jesus's blood redeemed—no curse
Sweat and toil are no longer tools
Prayer and worship is what we use
Weapons of war we now put to ground
Beaten swords now plow the land
Hope we sow and joy we reap
As every promise God does keep
Every seed brings forth fresh fruit
Our faithful God—devourers he rebukes
Nations and neighbors call us blessed
Our tithes in his storehouse give us rest
From windows of heaven—pour him down
We gather all brethren and share it around.

Reflect—Question—Ponder—Pray

We're called to be more than just us; we're called to be a blessing to the local communities and world around us. Our healing and growth should be having a positive influence and effect on all our relationships, and our employers and co-workers should feel the presence of Christ in us. God is a God of mutuality. He never does anything just for one person—even when he works on us personally, it's with the heart of us becoming a change agent for the good of others.

The Lord has built you up to be a blessing and a testimony in other people's lives. Ask him to lay the names of one or two people, whom you can pray for regularly. Ask him to show you how to encourage and be a better friend to them.

Amen

Treasure Hunt

A new life, a new beginning, a new start
A new adventure in the mystery of who you are
A new path littered with promises and grace
The same instruction to always seek your face
A new trust, a new faith, to step out in new ways
A new perspective of serving the ancient of days
A fresh anointing and cleansing and bathing in oil
A fresh desire to find the new places where you dwell.

Reflect—Question—Ponder—Pray

When the Lord has built us up sufficiently, healed us, and filled us with his truths and Word, the next thing he'll do is send us out into the world.

Change is an expected part of our Christian walk. Different jobs, careers, relationships, responsibilities, and even challenges are supposed to build up our knowledge of Christ. When we've taken hold of the lessons and principles God's been teaching us, he'll move us onto the next level. This will come with new challenges, but also new measures of grace, plus the opportunity to influence and impact other people's lives with the love of the Gospel.

The Bible tells us that although we are in the world, we are not of the world. We are in fact Christ's ambassadors on earth. It's a wonderful assignment; we get to be peacemakers and solution-bringers, and we provide the cohesion and compassion that builds unity and trust.

So, if you finally feel that you've got it all together and God comes along and mixes it all up . . . congratulations! He's promoting and trusting you with more.

Be encouraged, good and faithful servant.

FOLLOW ME THERE

Ah, you're so faithful and you want us the same—you don't want
us to get discouraged and quit the game
The race, you said, is not to the swift—time proves whether we
really believe in you and that faith uplifts
No abandoning of Rhema for a simpler life, no compromising
your vision to avoid trials and strife
No rejecting your instructions when we feel adrift—knowing in
the rage of the storms you're still in our midst
Faith is constructed in this —when we can't see the way and thus
we're only driven by what you say
Following a still voice—in a valley of taunts, looking for a candle
flame amongst shadows of fear and blame
Knowing you can never change, knowing you can never revoke
what you say, knowing you're the same
Pick up the cross, you say—the weight of it is the burden of
promise you bear
Lifting this up means dropping every other care
You'll find me on your way up there
I went first to prepare
I'll give you destiny for despair
Just pick up your cross, you say—
And follow me there
It will crucify every unbelief
It will reveal who I made you to be
Pick up your cross and follow me.

Reflect—Question—Ponder—Pray

What does this passage speak to you?

THERE'S NO COMFORT IN BEING GREAT

There's no comfort in being great
We're all being stretched . . .
At least it's not upon a cross
Not having to carry the weight of another's dross
Not bleeding to stem their loss
Not being beaten as part of their cost
We're stretched to receive; we're stretched to conceive
We're widening our hips and strengthening our grip
Creating room for something great
Creating space for the ancient of days
To step into our vessels and transform our dreams of clay
Into something that has never been conceived in our generation
or days
Make no mistake
This stretching it breaks
It tears away
There's no comfort in being great
The aching is because he's molding success
He's accelerating you and catapulting you through many tests
He's drawing out his best and scrapping off the rest
You will break
He's removing everything superficial and fake
Every tear and snare that would stand in his way
Authenticity is the hallmark of great
Make no mistake
Role-playing our God won't tolerate
Insecurity is the antithesis of faith
So he's shaking all those removable things away
Wake up and accept his ways
We can't kick against his grace
We can't wrestle with his truth
That truth is supposed to liberate you

It's just easier to obey you
To do what you say to do
To trust you
Trusting you is the hardest thing to do
In a life, in a world that betrays you
But then you know exactly what we're going through
You've been there too
I love how it always comes back to you
It's not easy being great . . .
I accept it, it's OK . . .
because you died to pave the way.
Amen

Reflect—Question—Ponder—Pray

This is a very sobering passage. Read it over. What did it say to you?

_____

_____

_____

_____

_____

Uncomfortably Expectant

When you've spoken, I will know
It won't come from thoughts of my own!
Won't be confusion or doubt
The gentleness of your voice
Will crowd out the noise
The stillness of your tone
Does quieten the soul
The conviction from within settles
So instruction can begin
You don't speak in vain
You don't throw out quips to brighten my day
Your Rhema brings enlightenment and change
And it's always in accordance with your written ways.

Reflect—Question—Ponder—Pray

We often don't recognize God's leading and speaking. There are many reasons for this: busyness, doubt, lack of confidence, skepticism, and fear. Be assured, when God speaks there is total peace. Even if what he is asking us to do is totally unheard of or foreign to us, there will still be peace. Nothing of God has fear, doom, or negative emotions attached to it. God never criticizes or condemns us. He equips us by sharing his heart and vision for our lives, and by showing us how to step into his best.

What do you feel God has said to you recently? How have you acted on his words?

Peace Without End

Where there's counsel and good friends
Your government of peace won't end
Where there's wisdom and insight
There's the knowledge of what's good and right
Where there's obedience and trust
There's your ever-flowing well of love
Where there's understanding and might
There's instruction in the depths of night
Where there's patience and hope
There's the manifestation of every word you spoke
Where there's worship and work
You make us your royal diadem in the earth
Where there's walking in your will
Your prophecy of Christ, in us, is fulfilled.

Reflect—Question—Ponder—Pray

We can't do this journey of purpose on our own. There are specific people and divine relationships that God has prepared for you. We should all have spiritual mentors—people with similar gifts and callings—who have walked the journey ahead of us; thus can help navigate and pass on timesaving knowledge from their own experiences.

Sometimes we already know these individuals, others we're yet to meet. Like Ruth and Naomi, and Jonathan and David, these are strategic spiritual partnerships that are keys to unlocking parts of our destiny. This is an individual appointed by God, not someone we choose based on rapport or feelings.

Ask the Lord to lead you to the people and the divine relationships he has purposed for your life. Ask him for the grace to recognize these individuals when they come along. (They're often not what we're expecting!) Ask him for the steadfastness to walk the journey to its end. Some people will be for life and others for a season, so you must always remain sensitive to the Holy Spirit's leading.

Amen

Papa

Let me always be in your presence found
Let my life song be upon sheets of grace
Let my emotions never leave the pages of your Word
Let provocation in me never be heard.

Let me be as meek as the dove and as humble as the lamb
That knows it needs the tending of a shepherd's hand
Let me be as trusting as the raven and as patient as the bud
Splendidly arrayed and clothed and fed in each new day
Let me be as complacent as the moon in its bowing to the sun
And as faithful as the stars who march out nightly, one by one
As obedient as the waves who won't transgress the shore, but stay
And like the serenity of a leaf and the stillness of the dew
Let me, gracious Father, be always found in you!

Reflect—Question—Ponder—Pray

Abiding in Christ is the heart, the pulse of the Christian walk. The things that God will allow us to experience and impact: the favors, miracles, and blessings can never be allowed to become more important or attractive than God himself. He is the source of all things. And he alone deserves all our adoration and praise.

Notes:

_____

_____

_____

God's Thoughts Define Me!

WHEN WE KNOW WHO God made us to be and why, we become unstoppable. We can shake off and bat away every lie, every false word, and every attack, because we know what we're about.

When you realize you're an eagle, you'll start turning down invitations to the chicken coop. When you know what God has purposed you for, you'll stop running around in relationships that move you in the opposite direction. When you become aware of the treasure the Lord has deposited in you, you'll stop hiring yourself out as cheap labor and start investing in yourself instead of being a consumer of the world.

Purpose and destiny begin when you start to let God's thoughts, words, and opinions define you. When you believe what God says about you; when you walk in the authority and dominion Christ has given you; when you determine in your spirit and soul that there is nothing of worth the world or the devil can offer you, you've stepped into your purpose. Being who Christ made you to be is the greatest achievement you could ever have on this earth.

Coming into direct alignment with God like this—feeding on his Word, letting his identity coarse through your veins, holding everything up to the light of what he says about you—is the key to the victorious and abundant life Christ died to give you.

God's thoughts define you!
Hallelujah and Amen!

Shake It Off

Shake off the dust, shake off the crowd
Leave their tattered opinions on the ground
Merchants and pushers of oppressive ideals
Trading God's glory, bruising his heel
Forgetting the devil came to steal and kill
Exposing the very wounds Christ came to heal
Not ashamed of forgetting, but afraid to yield.

Shake off their appraisals—they're the braying crowd
The ones that shouted, "If he's God, he'll let himself down"
The ones that twisted his thorny crown
They're always ever so loud . . .
But when you need a faithful witness, they're never around
When you need forgiveness, they've taken stones from the
ground.

Shake off their dust and find higher ground
On the mount of transfiguration is where we ought to be found.

Don't dip your bread or consume of their meat
Shake off their dust and let God wash your feet
It's only Christ's words that make us complete
The vitriol of scorners only leads to defeat
Open his Word and look for your worth
He spoke your very existence from the dust of his earth
Godly treasure in vessels of clay
Let him speak the words that put mediocracy away
Wonderfully and fearfully and thoughtfully made
Will you let his words define who you are from this day?

It's time to move on and cut loose the shackles of other people's opinions and views about you. It's time to move up. God wants to elevate you to the position of an eagle, where you'll have perspective and understanding concerning all the things around you. But when you're caught up in the opinions and appraisals of the world, you're like a chicken in a coop, flapping and flapping but never getting off the ground.

Never look at it as turning your back on people, more of turning yourself and your full focus and attention to God.

Thoughts:

_____

_____

_____

_____

_____

OUTWORKING SALVATION

None you'd ever turn away; you sent your son to reveal your
name
He shed his blood for all to claim—to wipe them clean from sin
and blame
To clothe them in his righteous threads, and place dominion on
their heads
To lift the sick from off their beds, and cast out all life's fears and
dreads
You raise the weak and feed the poor, and lock the violent man
out the door
You hold the keys to heaven's stores and pour abundant life, and
more
Your crowning joy is our soothing oil, which washes all our daily
toil
Our identity, Christ, is in you—your presence fills our every
room
Help us surrender to you, and show you praise in all we do.

Reflect—Question—Ponder—Pray

We are built up, mended, and made whole so that we can carry God's glory and light into the world. The Bible tells us we're supposed to do more miracles and greater exploits than Jesus. Wow . . . what an offer, what an incredible opportunity to be used by God to bring hope, joy, healing, and liberation!

God cares for all humanity. He loves non-Christians just as much as he loves us; and he wants us all to live free from evil, oppression, illness, injustice, and darkness. God chose you to be his representative to the world around you.

How are you going to tap into God's grace in order to rise to this challenge?

_____

_____

_____

_____

_____

_____

Are there certain global or societal issues that you're willing to take up in prayer?

_____

_____

_____

_____

_____

THE CARELESS

The lost know not from where they're clothed or fed
They think existence comes from their heads
Not knowing they live on your very life breath
Not knowing your precious blood was shed
Help us shine, Lord, in their unbelief
So through our lives for you they'll seek
Your wisdom, let them hear us speak
To know that they've been made unique
And have eternity at your feet
Help us be your salt and light
And always in love fight the good fight
Salvation, Lord, belongs to all—help us bring to them your call!

Reflect—Question—Ponder—Pray

God chose us for this purpose.

Jesus called each of his disciples by name; he didn't just command them to believe—no, he walked, ate, talked, debated, and wept with them. Above all, he showed them all love. They didn't just believe by his words, but by how he lived.

The first Epistle of John speaks of what they had heard, seen, and looked upon, and what their hands had handled concerning Christ. These were the elements of their testimony; their witness came not just from what they saw, but from what they experienced.

The same is true of us; it is your experience of Christ that will draw others to him.

Thoughts:

_____

_____

_____

_____

Ask the Lord how he can make your career, parenting, or business
a testimony for his glory, salvation, and love.

   In Jesus's name,

   Amen

Enlarge Your Tent

Stepping out in action in faith is faith
There's no need to be afraid of making mistakes
Carrying that name, Jesus, it always subdues
And it's the banner we carry in everything we do
If faith without works is dead, then we must stop deliberating and
take action instead!
You said your righteous will not see shame—so let's pray then
step forth in Jesus's name!

Smarten us, Father, to be sensitive to you—
Let us know your heart before we do what we do
Strengthen us to follow the convictions of your Word
Filter out the strange voices and lies that we've heard.

Let us be like tender clay—we are the vessel that you have made
Let us flow in streams of grace—and not be found in opposing
ways
Let us worship and revere—you are the God that draweth near
Let us take the narrow gate—and not compromise our walk of
faith!

Keep us holy and keep us in truth—we need to surrender our all
to you
Teach us the beauty of seeking you in prayer—and receiving the
assurance that you always care
Rescue us from trouble with your mighty arms—and let us see
how you're our foundation when all isn't calm
Teach us to fear and revere your name—you're sovereign,
righteous, holy, and without number of days
Tutor us in becoming students of light—your Word is the
illumination that ignites and gives life.

Reflect—Question—Ponder—Pray

We're going to pray for boldness, courage, and strength. The boldness to act in faith, the courage to take God at his Word, and the strength to persevere until we see his promises come through.

Enlarging your tent means stepping out in action in faith. What faith actions can you start taking from today?

_____

_____

_____

_____

FEET FIGHT

In fulfilling your purpose we will be complete
In walking our destiny is rest for our feet
Pre-known, pre-destined, and pre-called
There was a reason you birthed us all
There's a place in our souls that will never be satisfied
Unless we're living your purpose for our lives
Instead of just existing in a menagerie of disguise
Held captive to worldly thoughts and soul-destroying lies
Your treasure of glory in our jars of clay
Will never consciously stop tugging away
Waiting to be released, discovered, and explained
So it can express the majesty of the ancient of days
So let's fall on our knees and to our Heavenly Father exclaim
Let your glory and power in me be displayed
You wrote about me in your book of life—Oh merciful Father,
breathe each letter alive
Give me the obedience to overcome strife
Give me the discipline to walk in your light
Let me be submissive in heeding your Word
Let me be compliant when from you I've heard
Send me companions, mentors, and friends
I'm committing to walk this journey, in its fullness, to its end.
Amen

Reflect—Question—Ponder—Pray

What gifts and creativity do you possess that you are not using?
Why not?

_____

_____

_____

_____

What steps can you take to start using them?

_____

_____

_____

_____

_____

What are you waiting for? Time to get started!

Your Thoughts Define Me

Your thoughts define me
The very warmth of your breath lives inside me
Your fingerprints are on my flesh and bones
You gathered me together when you first spoke
Created in your image, with no burden or yoke
"It was very good," echoes through my soul
"It was very good," is all I need to know.

Fearfully and wonderfully made is no slogan or joke
It's what causes every curse and false judgement to be revoked
It's a declaration that is blood bought and blood soaked
It causes every weapon and strategy of the enemy to go up in
smoke.

You led captivity captive—you made hell go broke
Capturing souls by the love that you spoke
Bridging the gap by exposing your flesh
Pouring yourself out—rendering your best
Gathering your creations—little lambs to your flock
Not a single one is missing—you paid for the whole lot.

You thoughts define me
They mold me like clay
In your hands I can excel a million different ways
The warmth from your palms—smooths all that was rough
The warmth of your heart is your eternal love.

Reflect—Question—Ponder—Pray

Reread the passage and write down all the thoughts about your
identity that the Lord is going to drop into your soul. He's talking
to you right now.

Pen Of A Ready Writer

You told me to sit down and write
You told me in words was a fight
A battle of what's wrong versus what's right
Words that ignite with spirit and sword
To cut asunder and break death's cords
Like flames to the stubble on the threshing floor
Are the words of a prophet sent straight from the Lord!
Your words are the power that cause waves to stand
And humble the haughty and exalt the poor man
Your words are the substance that formed us from clay
Your words caused the fig tree to wither away
Your words stripped the darkness and gave sight to the blind
And that word repentance restores mankind.
Your kingdom come, these words be done
In the earth to which you sent your son.

Reflect—Question—Ponder—Pray

The Lord told me to sit down and write, and the result is the very book you're reading now. What has God put on the inside of you? You have to know that it's your God-given right and identity to grow into the fullness of your purpose. Ask the Lord to reveal all that he's placed within you.

There are things inside you that God wants to use to change lives and bless communities, even nations. We, the body of Christ, the world at large, need those things. This means we need you to be all that God designed and created you to be. No one else can offer the world what you can.

What has God put inside you?

All Need You

Bring all people to your throne
So your grace, O God, they'll know
Let us be your willing hands
So the lost may understand
Let your spirit work within
So repentance can begin
So confession can take part
Of Lord Jesus, from their heart
So your kingdom will, will shine
In their thoughts and in their minds
In your power from on high
Pour out your eternal life.

Reflect—Question—Ponder—Pray

I believe the first step to living a transformed life is recognizing and acknowledging that we are not Christians by our own conclusion or intelligence. It wasn't a mental decision to choose Christ; it was his power and mercy that opened our hearts and minds to accept him. When we come to fully believe it was all down to him, we'll stop looking at non-Christians as if they've stupidly made the wrong choice.

When we understand the only difference that separates us is God's sovereignty, we will be more compassionate, tolerant, and eager to show the same fruits of love that we were given.

Take the time to search your heart and see if you're carrying any form of pride or arrogance because you're a Christian. Ask the Lord for forgiveness and to replace these feelings with humility and the knowledge of his heart and love towards all his creations.

In Jesus's name,

Amen

COMMISSIONED

The free gift of a fresh start and a righteousness that cannot
depart
O glorious Father, how mighty art thou works
A broken flower in your hand—your tender heart does make to
stand
O glorious Father, how compassionate is your love
The dove that lost her song of trust—the soul that's fallen in the
dust
O glorious Father, your Word of truth restores
The bottles full of bitter tears—the sobs that fell on deafened ears
O healing Father, our faithful judge avenge
The misplaced purpose in the dark—the body bruised with
mistakes and scars
O healing Father, in resurrection power ignite
The widow begging in the street, the orphans' needs that run soul
deep
O sovereign Father, make us be their light
Send us, Father, in your might
Salt us with your shield and fight
Help us cast out dark and night
That your kingdom will shine bright
Put the truth of Christ in sight
Let them see him in our lives
Occupy our hearts and minds
Let our actions testify
That the Word of God is nigh!

Reflect—Question—Ponder—Pray

What do you think your responsibilities are, as a Christian, to
humanity?

INTENTIONAL

Let's take up our armor of brotherly love, and by our captain,
Lord Jesus above . . .
March into territories of injustice and abuse, take over
strongholds, and set people loose
Let's level the mountains, as fine as the dust, let's cast out the
demons with their evil lusts
Let's march in the glory of Jehovah Gibbor, and tear down the
walls and beat down death's doors
Let's decree and declare with shield, sword, and bow—that the
enemy must let God's people *Grow*!
We won't stand for torment and be daily accused, we won't let
deception buffet and bruise
We won't see corruption and turn our heads away, because we've
become too weak to intercede and pray!
We are Christ's body—a mighty army of many parts! And at the
name of Jesus, demons do depart!
You said if we believe and are called by your name —we will put
devils, rulers, and principalities to shame
Bind up the strongman and plunder his goods—it's only to you,
Lord Jesus, we have to look
Lord, you've written all the endings in your glorious book!
We're rising in victory, we're shouting out, "No!" Coz every
manipulation and oppression has to go
Your kingdom's principles through us must flow—so we're letting
every captive know . . .
That the anointing which breaks yokes has started to flow—we
will fulfil our duty to bring those lost home
We will be your hands, Lord, your heart, eyes, and feet—knowing
that led by your spirit there is no defeat.

Reflect—Question—Ponder—Pray

This, my friends, is why God has chosen us as Christians. We must all mature and walk in our full purposes, diligently seeking the Lord in intercession and prayer for our communities and the world. We must be determined to grow in our relationship with God and to continue to operate in humility, tolerance, forgiveness, and love. Knowing we carry the very power of Christ inside us, knowing that power has the ability to transform societies, governments, and nations.

Thank you so much for choosing to stand up and be counted; heaven applauds you, I applaud you, the companies, nations, and societies that will be positively impacted by you stepping into all that God has designed you to be, applauds you. May our Lord and Savior, Jesus Christ, preserve, uphold, and sustain all you do in his mighty name.

God bless!

Afterword

THANK YOU SO MUCH again for journeying with me—I hope you were enlightened, encouraged, and feel purposed. God is continually speaking, instructing, and directing us and as his children, we have full access to heaven's divine wisdom, and more.

May you forever dwell in the knowledge of Christ's love for you.

Sincerely,

Asisat

BLOG

https://thechristiancommute.blogspot.com

CPSIA information can be obtained
at www.ICGtesting.com
Printed in the USA
LVHW082343180122
708881LV00013B/319